All About Taj Mahal: A Kid's Guide to India's Most Famous Monument

Educational Books For Kids, Volume 4

Shah Rukh

Published by Shah Rukh, 2024.

While every precaution has been taken in the preparation of this book, the publisher assumes no responsibility for errors or omissions, or for damages resulting from the use of the information contained herein.

ALL ABOUT TAJ MAHAL: A KID'S GUIDE TO INDIA'S MOST FAMOUS MONUMENT

First edition. September 16, 2024.

Copyright © 2024 Shah Rukh.

ISBN: 979-8227202161

Written by Shah Rukh.

Table of Contents

Prologue

Welcome to an incredible journey to one of the most beautiful and famous monuments in the world – the Taj Mahal! This book is your special guide to uncovering all the amazing secrets, stories, and facts about this magnificent structure. Built hundreds of years ago, the Taj Mahal isn't just a building; it's a symbol of love, beauty, and history that has fascinated people for centuries.

Imagine a palace so grand, it looks like it's floating on clouds, with walls that change color as the sun rises and sets. Imagine being able to explore the gardens, the towers, and the river that flows beside it. Now, get ready to step into the world of Mughal emperors, discover the love story that inspired the Taj Mahal, and find out why people from all over the world still visit this breathtaking site.

As we travel through time and space, you'll learn about how the Taj Mahal was built, the people who created it, and the legends that surround it. You'll even get to discover some hidden details and fun facts that most people might miss! Whether you're visiting the Taj Mahal for the first time or exploring it from the comfort of your home, this book will make sure you know everything there is to know about India's most famous monument.

So, buckle up and get ready to dive into the fascinating world of the Taj Mahal. It's going to be an adventure you won't forget!

Chapter 1: The Love Story Behind the Taj Mahal

The Taj Mahal, one of the most magnificent and iconic structures in the world, was born out of an extraordinary love story. This grand monument is not just a stunning example of architectural brilliance, but it stands as a symbol of eternal love, grief, and remembrance. The love story behind the Taj Mahal centers around Shah Jahan, the fifth Mughal emperor of India, and his beloved wife, Mumtaz Mahal, whose untimely death inspired him to build this enduring masterpiece.

Shah Jahan, born as Prince Khurram in 1592, was the son of Emperor Jahangir and the grandson of Akbar the Great. As a young man, he was well-known for his intelligence, charm, and military prowess. In 1607, at the age of 15, Prince Khurram met Arjumand Banu Begum, a Persian princess of exceptional beauty and grace. She was the granddaughter of a powerful Persian noble and the daughter of Asaf Khan, who held high positions in the Mughal court. The young prince was immediately captivated by her beauty and elegance, and the two fell deeply in love.

Though they were engaged soon after their meeting, their marriage did not take place until five years later, in 1612. When they finally married, Arjumand Banu Begum became known as Mumtaz Mahal, which means "Jewel of the Palace" in Persian, a title befitting her status as the emperor's most cherished wife. Their relationship was marked by profound affection, respect, and devotion. Shah Jahan and Mumtaz Mahal shared an unbreakable bond, and she became his most trusted companion and advisor, accompanying him on military campaigns and standing by his side in all matters of state.

Mumtaz Mahal was not only a devoted wife but also a mother of 14 children, although only seven survived into adulthood. Despite the demanding responsibilities of motherhood, she remained the constant companion of Shah Jahan. Their love for each other was celebrated throughout the Mughal Empire, with Shah Jahan often referring to her as his soulmate. Mumtaz Mahal was known for her compassion and kindness, and she played a significant role in the lives of the people around her, engaging in charitable work and advocating for the welfare of women and the poor.

Tragically, their love story took a heart-wrenching turn in 1631, when Mumtaz Mahal passed away while giving birth to their 14th child. She had accompanied Shah Jahan on a military campaign in the Deccan plateau, as she often did, despite being pregnant. After giving birth to their daughter, Gauharara Begum, Mumtaz Mahal fell gravely ill and, despite the best efforts of the imperial doctors, she died in Shah Jahan's arms. Her death devastated the emperor. Overwhelmed with grief, Shah Jahan was inconsolable, and it is said that he withdrew from public life for a time, mourning the loss of the woman who had been the center of his world.

In the depths of his sorrow, Shah Jahan resolved to build a monument that would serve as an eternal tribute to Mumtaz Mahal, one that would commemorate their love and her memory for generations to come. He envisioned a structure so beautiful and majestic that it would be unparalleled in the world. Thus, the idea for the Taj Mahal was born, a mausoleum that would house the remains of Mumtaz Mahal and stand as a testament to their undying love.

The construction of the Taj Mahal began in 1632, just a year after Mumtaz Mahal's death. Shah Jahan spared no expense in ensuring that the monument would be the most exquisite architectural achievement of its time. The emperor enlisted the finest artisans, craftsmen, and architects from across the Mughal Empire, as well as from Persia, Central Asia, and beyond, to bring his vision to life. Ustad Ahmad Lahauri, a renowned architect from Persia, is widely believed to have been the principal designer of the Taj Mahal.

The construction took more than 20 years to complete, with over 20,000 laborers working tirelessly to build the mausoleum and its surrounding complex. The Taj Mahal was built using white marble, quarried from Makrana in Rajasthan, which was chosen for its pristine beauty and ability to reflect the changing light of day. The shimmering marble was inlaid with precious and semi-precious stones, such as jasper, jade, turquoise, lapis lazuli, and amethyst, creating intricate floral designs and geometric patterns that added to the monument's ethereal beauty.

The Taj Mahal's central dome rises majestically above the structure, flanked by four smaller domes and four slender minarets at each corner of the platform. The symmetry and balance of the design reflect the Mughal architectural style, which was heavily influenced by Persian, Islamic, and Indian traditions. At the heart of the Taj Mahal is the tomb of Mumtaz Mahal, which lies directly beneath the main dome. Her sarcophagus is surrounded by a delicate marble screen, intricately carved with floral motifs and Quranic inscriptions. Shah Jahan's tomb was later added beside hers after his death in 1666, though his tomb is placed asymmetrically, breaking the otherwise perfect symmetry of the design.

The Taj Mahal complex also includes a beautiful garden, designed in the traditional Persian charbagh layout, which is divided into four quadrants by water channels. The garden symbolizes paradise, reflecting the Islamic concept of the afterlife, where rivers flow through lush gardens. The reflection of the Taj Mahal in the pools of water adds to its enchanting allure, making it appear as though the monument is floating on air.

Throughout the years, the Taj Mahal has been regarded as a symbol of the deep and enduring love between Shah Jahan and Mumtaz Mahal. It represents not only the grief of a husband who lost his beloved wife but also the lengths to which he went to immortalize her memory. For centuries, the story of their love has captivated people from all corners of the globe, and the Taj Mahal continues to stand as one of the most beautiful and poignant expressions of love in human history.

Shah Jahan's devotion to Mumtaz Mahal did not end with the construction of the Taj Mahal. After her death, he continued to visit her tomb, and it is said that he could often be found gazing upon the Taj Mahal from a distance, lost in memories of their time together. However, Shah Jahan's later years were marked by further tragedy. In 1658, his son Aurangzeb seized power in a coup and imprisoned his father in the Agra Fort, where Shah Jahan spent the last eight years of his life. From his prison cell, he had a view of the Taj Mahal, a bittersweet reminder of his lost love. When Shah Jahan passed away in 1666, he was buried beside Mumtaz Mahal, fulfilling his wish to be reunited with her in death.

The love story behind the Taj Mahal is not just a story of romantic love, but also one of loss, devotion, and the desire to preserve the memory of a loved one for eternity. It is a tale that transcends time and has resonated with people of all cultures and backgrounds. The Taj Mahal is often called the "monument of love," and it continues to inspire awe and admiration as one of the most iconic and beautiful structures in the world. Its enduring legacy is a reminder of the power of love and the lengths to which one can go to honor the memory of a beloved companion. The monument's beauty, coupled with the poignant story behind it, ensures that the Taj Mahal will forever remain a symbol of love's timeless and transcendent nature.

Chapter 2: How the Taj Mahal Was Built

The construction of the Taj Mahal is a remarkable tale of architectural ingenuity, painstaking craftsmanship, and sheer human determination. Built in the mid-17th century, this iconic monument stands not only as a testament to love but also as a masterwork of Mughal architecture, blending Persian, Islamic, and Indian styles into a singular expression of beauty. The story of how the Taj Mahal was built begins with Emperor Shah Jahan's grief over the death of his beloved wife, Mumtaz Mahal, and his vision of a mausoleum that would eternally honor her memory. From its conception to its completion, the building process of the Taj Mahal was an unparalleled feat of artistry and engineering.

After the death of Mumtaz Mahal in 1631, Shah Jahan was devastated and immediately began planning a mausoleum that would reflect the beauty and grandeur of his lost queen. He envisioned a monument unlike anything the world had seen before, one that would stand for centuries as a symbol of their love. The emperor's dream was to build a tomb that was as magnificent as it was permanent. Thus, he assembled the best minds of his time, bringing together architects, artisans, and engineers from across the Mughal Empire and beyond. Craftsmen from Persia, the Ottoman Empire, and Europe were invited to contribute their skills to the creation of the Taj Mahal.

The design of the Taj Mahal is often attributed to Ustad Ahmad Lahauri, a Persian architect known for his work on other significant Mughal projects. However, it is widely believed that a team of architects collaborated on the design, blending various architectural styles and techniques. The construction process officially began in 1632, a year after Mumtaz Mahal's death, and it would take more than two decades to complete. The Taj Mahal complex, which includes the main mausoleum, a mosque, a guest house, gardens, and a series of gates, was constructed in phases, with the main mausoleum taking approximately 12 years to finish.

The first step in the building process was to select the site for the Taj Mahal. Shah Jahan chose a location on the banks of the Yamuna River in Agra, a city that had been the capital of the Mughal Empire since the reign of his grandfather, Emperor Akbar. The site was chosen not only for its proximity to Agra Fort, where Shah Jahan ruled, but also because the river provided a serene and reflective setting for the monument. The Yamuna River also played a practical role in the construction, as it allowed for the easy transportation of materials to the site.

Once the site was chosen, the ground had to be prepared. Since the land along the river was prone to flooding, the foundation of the Taj Mahal had to be fortified to ensure its stability. Workers drove large wooden piles deep into the earth to create a stable base, and the foundation was then filled with rubble and covered with layers of stone to provide a solid platform for the structure. It is said that a well-planned system of wells was also dug to drain any excess water from the area, preventing future flooding from damaging the foundation.

The construction materials used in the Taj Mahal were sourced from all over India and beyond, reflecting the vast reach and wealth of the Mughal Empire. The most prominent material used in the construction was white marble, which gives the Taj Mahal its distinctive and ethereal appearance. The marble was quarried from Makrana, a town in the Indian state of Rajasthan, located several hundred miles away from Agra. Transporting the heavy marble slabs to the construction site was no small feat. Elephants, oxen, and carts were used to move the stones, and it is believed that a specially constructed system of ramps made of earth and bricks helped lift the marble into place during construction.

In addition to marble, a wide variety of other materials were used to decorate and adorn the Taj Mahal. The white marble was inlaid with precious and semi-precious stones such as jade, crystal, turquoise, lapis lazuli, amethyst, and coral, sourced from places as far away as China,

Sri Lanka, and Afghanistan. These stones were intricately cut and set into the marble using a technique known as pietra dura, a form of inlay work that was mastered by the Mughal artisans. The floral and geometric patterns created through pietra dura add a rich and delicate ornamentation to the monument, giving the Taj Mahal its detailed and luxurious appearance.

The construction of the main mausoleum, which stands at the center of the Taj Mahal complex, began with the creation of the large, square platform on which it rests. This platform elevates the mausoleum and ensures that it dominates the surrounding landscape. The platform is also surrounded by four slender minarets, one at each corner, which add to the symmetry and grandeur of the structure. Each minaret was carefully designed and built with a slight outward tilt, so that in the event of an earthquake, the minarets would fall away from the main tomb, rather than collapsing onto it.

The main tomb itself is an octagonal structure topped with a massive central dome that rises to a height of 240 feet. The dome, made of marble, is often described as onion-shaped, and it is one of the most striking features of the Taj Mahal. The dome's graceful curvature and height give the monument its sense of weightlessness, as though it is floating above the landscape. The engineering required to construct such a dome was advanced for its time, and it is a testament to the skill of the architects and builders. The dome is crowned with a gilded finial, which combines Islamic and Hindu elements, reflecting the syncretic nature of Mughal architecture.

Inside the main mausoleum lies the tomb of Mumtaz Mahal, which is placed at the center of the structure directly beneath the central dome. Her cenotaph, or empty tomb, is surrounded by a delicate marble screen, known as a jali, which is intricately carved with floral patterns and Quranic inscriptions. The real tomb of Mumtaz Mahal lies in a crypt below the main chamber, as is customary in Islamic burial practices. After Shah Jahan's death in 1666, he was also buried in the

Taj Mahal, and his cenotaph was placed beside that of Mumtaz Mahal, slightly offset to the west, breaking the otherwise perfect symmetry of the design.

While the main mausoleum is the most famous part of the Taj Mahal, the construction of the entire complex was a massive undertaking that involved the coordination of numerous workers, materials, and techniques. It is estimated that more than 20,000 laborers, artisans, and craftsmen were employed in the construction, working under the supervision of master architects and engineers. In addition to local workers, skilled craftsmen from Persia, Central Asia, and Europe were brought in to contribute their expertise in fields such as stone carving, inlay work, calligraphy, and mosaic making.

The Taj Mahal complex includes several other important structures that were built simultaneously with the mausoleum. To the west of the mausoleum stands a mosque, made of red sandstone and marble, which serves as a place of worship for those visiting the tomb. The mosque's design is similar to other Mughal mosques of the time, with a large central iwan, or prayer hall, flanked by smaller domed chambers. To the east of the mausoleum is a guest house, which was likely intended to accommodate visitors to the Taj Mahal. Like the mosque, the guest house is also built of red sandstone and features a design that complements the symmetry and balance of the overall complex.

Another significant aspect of the Taj Mahal's construction is its surrounding garden, which was designed in the traditional Persian charbagh style. The charbagh garden is divided into four quadrants by raised walkways and water channels, symbolizing the rivers of paradise in Islamic cosmology. The lush greenery, flowering plants, and reflective pools create a serene and peaceful atmosphere that enhances the beauty of the monument. The garden plays an important role in the overall design of the Taj Mahal, as it was intended to represent a paradise on Earth, where Shah Jahan could be reunited with Mumtaz Mahal in the afterlife.

In addition to the garden and the mausoleum, the Taj Mahal complex is accessed through a grand entrance gate made of red sandstone and marble. This gate, known as the Darwaza-i-Rauza, features intricate calligraphy and floral designs, and it serves as a symbolic threshold between the mundane world outside and the heavenly world inside the Taj Mahal. The symmetry and proportionality of the gate, like the rest of the complex, reflects the Mughal emphasis on balance and order in their architecture.

The construction of the Taj Mahal was a massive logistical operation that required careful planning and coordination. Supplies of marble, stone, and other materials were transported to the site using an elaborate network of roads, rivers, and canals. Workers lived in temporary settlements around the site, where they were housed and fed by the royal treasury. The construction process also involved the use of advanced building techniques, such as the use of wooden scaffolding and pulleys to raise heavy stones into place, and the employment of hydraulic systems to manage the flow of water in the garden.

Despite the challenges and complexity of the project, the Taj Mahal was completed within a relatively short period of time for a structure of its scale and intricacy. The main mausoleum was completed around 1643, but work on the surrounding buildings, gardens, and finishing touches continued for several more years. The entire complex was completed by 1653, nearly 22 years after construction began. The result was a breathtaking monument that has since become one of the most recognized and admired structures in the world, attracting millions of visitors each year.

The construction of the Taj Mahal was not just a technical achievement, but also a cultural and artistic one. It represents the pinnacle of Mughal architecture, blending elements of Persian, Islamic, and Indian design into a harmonious whole. The intricate craftsmanship and attention to detail that went into every aspect of its construction have made the Taj Mahal a masterpiece of human creativity, and its enduring beauty continues to inspire awe and admiration today.

Chapter 3: The Life of Shah Jahan

Shah Jahan, born as Prince Khurram on January 5, 1592, was one of the most significant rulers of the Mughal Empire, reigning from 1628 to 1658. His reign is often regarded as the golden age of Mughal architecture and culture, primarily because of the majestic monuments he commissioned, most notably the Taj Mahal, which stands as a testament to his deep love for his wife, Mumtaz Mahal. The life of Shah Jahan was marked by opulence, power, military conquest, personal tragedy, and eventually, a dramatic fall from power. His legacy, however, is inseparably tied to the grandeur and glory of the Mughal Empire during the 17th century.

Shah Jahan was the son of the Mughal Emperor Jahangir and his Rajput wife, Princess Manmati. His early years were filled with the typical luxuries and education expected of a Mughal prince. He was rigorously trained in the arts of war, administration, and the rich cultural heritage of the empire. His grandfather, Emperor Akbar, laid the foundation of the empire's vast and stable administration, and young Khurram was groomed to follow in this tradition. As he matured, he demonstrated exceptional talent in both military strategy and statesmanship, which earned him favor with his father, Emperor Jahangir, and the Mughal court.

As a young prince, Shah Jahan distinguished himself on several military campaigns, displaying both tactical brilliance and raw courage. His early exploits in the Deccan and other parts of India won him the admiration of both his father and the army. These campaigns were crucial in solidifying Mughal control over territories that were either rebellious or difficult to manage. Shah Jahan's military success bolstered his standing as a capable leader and a worthy successor to the Mughal throne, ensuring his place in the empire's future.

One of the most defining aspects of Shah Jahan's life was his marriage to Arjumand Banu Begum, who would later become known as Mumtaz Mahal. Their love story is one of the most romanticized and enduring tales in Indian history. They were married in 1612, and despite Shah Jahan having other wives, Mumtaz Mahal was his true love and constant companion. She accompanied him on his military campaigns and bore him fourteen children, though only seven survived infancy. The deep emotional bond they shared became legendary, especially after her untimely death in 1631 during the birth of their last child. Shah Jahan's grief at her passing was profound, and it was in her memory that he commissioned the construction of the Taj Mahal, a monument of love that would immortalize their relationship for centuries to come.

Before ascending to the throne, Shah Jahan had to navigate the complex and often treacherous politics of the Mughal court. Following the death of his father, Emperor Jahangir, in 1627, a brief but intense succession struggle ensued. Shah Jahan emerged victorious, thanks to his strategic alliances, military strength, and the support of influential nobles and courtiers. Once he became emperor in 1628, Shah Jahan set about consolidating his power and ensuring the stability of the empire. His reign, lasting thirty years, is often seen as a high point in the history of the Mughal Empire, marked by prosperity, cultural flourishing, and territorial expansion.

Shah Jahan's reign was characterized by his ambitious military campaigns, aimed at expanding and consolidating the empire's borders. He conducted successful campaigns in the Deccan region, consolidating Mughal control over the wealthy and strategically important territories of the south. He also turned his attention to Central Asia, seeking to reclaim the ancestral homelands of the Mughals in Samarkand and beyond, although these campaigns met with limited success. His expansionist policies also extended to the northwest, where he fought the Persians over control of Kandahar, a key region in modern-day Afghanistan. Despite setbacks in some areas,

Shah Jahan's military campaigns generally strengthened the Mughal Empire's position as a dominant power in the Indian subcontinent.

One of Shah Jahan's most enduring legacies is his patronage of the arts, particularly architecture. Under his reign, Mughal architecture reached its zenith, blending Persian, Indian, and Islamic styles into a unique aesthetic that has captivated the world for centuries. The most famous of these architectural achievements is, of course, the Taj Mahal, a mausoleum built for Mumtaz Mahal. However, Shah Jahan's architectural achievements extend far beyond the Taj Mahal. He also commissioned the construction of the Red Fort in Delhi, a massive complex that served as the seat of Mughal power, and the Jama Masjid, one of the largest and most beautiful mosques in India. Additionally, he oversaw the building of several palaces, gardens, and public works projects, transforming the landscape of Mughal cities into a vision of opulence and elegance.

The construction of these monumental structures required vast resources, and Shah Jahan's reign was marked by a flourishing economy that could support such grand projects. The Mughal Empire during his rule was one of the wealthiest and most powerful in the world, with a sophisticated system of taxation and trade that ensured a steady flow of revenue to the imperial treasury. Agriculture, which formed the backbone of the empire's economy, thrived during his reign, thanks to effective administrative policies and irrigation projects that improved the productivity of the land. Trade with Europe, Persia, and Central Asia also flourished, bringing exotic goods and wealth into the empire. This economic prosperity allowed Shah Jahan to maintain a large army, build magnificent structures, and live a life of extraordinary luxury.

Despite the success and grandeur of his reign, Shah Jahan's later years were marred by personal tragedy and political turmoil. The death of Mumtaz Mahal in 1631 profoundly affected him, and he increasingly withdrew from the day-to-day affairs of the empire, focusing more on completing the Taj Mahal and other architectural projects. His grief was so deep that he is said to have gone into a prolonged period of mourning, which led to his physical health deteriorating. As his health declined, his ability to effectively govern the empire waned, and he increasingly relied on his sons to manage the empire's affairs.

Shah Jahan's sons, most notably Dara Shikoh and Aurangzeb, became embroiled in a fierce succession struggle as their father's health worsened. Although Shah Jahan favored his eldest son, Dara Shikoh, to succeed him, the other princes were not willing to accept this decision without a fight. This led to a brutal and bloody civil war between the brothers. Aurangzeb, a shrewd and ruthless military leader, ultimately emerged victorious, defeating Dara Shikoh and imprisoning Shah Jahan in the Agra Fort in 1658. Shah Jahan spent the final years of his life under house arrest, confined to a small section of the fort where he could see the Taj Mahal from his window. This cruel twist of fate—being imprisoned by his own son and forced to live out his days gazing at the monument he built for his beloved wife—marks a tragic end to his life.

Shah Jahan's imprisonment lasted eight years, during which time he was allowed little contact with the outside world. He was cared for by his devoted daughter, Jahanara Begum, who remained loyal to him throughout his captivity. Despite his diminished status, Shah Jahan was still treated with respect, and his quarters in the Agra Fort were relatively comfortable, though a far cry from the grandeur he had once enjoyed as emperor. He spent his days reflecting on his life, his empire, and his lost love, while Aurangzeb consolidated his power as the new emperor.

Shah Jahan died on January 22, 1666, at the age of 74. His body was interred in the Taj Mahal, alongside Mumtaz Mahal, fulfilling his wish to be reunited with her in death. The final resting place of Shah Jahan and Mumtaz Mahal is located in the lower chamber of the Taj Mahal, where their graves lie next to each other, a poignant reminder of the love story that inspired one of the world's greatest architectural achievements.

Shah Jahan's legacy is a complex one. On one hand, he is remembered as a great patron of the arts, a visionary ruler who left behind some of the most beautiful and enduring monuments in the world. His reign marked a high point in Mughal culture, art, and architecture, and the Taj Mahal remains one of the most famous and beloved buildings on the planet. On the other hand, his later years were marked by political instability and the brutal succession struggle that ultimately led to his downfall. The empire that Shah Jahan left behind was still strong, but the seeds of its eventual decline had already been sown, particularly with the rise of Aurangzeb, whose conservative and authoritarian rule would alienate many of the empire's subjects.

Nevertheless, Shah Jahan's reign is often seen as the last great chapter in the history of the Mughal Empire. His vision of a vast, cosmopolitan, and culturally rich empire was realized during his lifetime, even if it would later unravel in the years following his death. Today, Shah Jahan is remembered not only for his achievements as a ruler but also for the incredible monuments he left behind, especially the Taj Mahal, which continues to inspire awe, admiration, and a sense of timeless beauty.

Chapter 4: The Beauty of Mughal Architecture

Mughal architecture is one of the most splendid and iconic forms of art and architectural style that flourished in the Indian subcontinent during the Mughal Empire, from the early 16th to the mid-18th century. It is a remarkable fusion of Islamic, Persian, Turkish, and Indian architectural elements, creating a distinctive aesthetic that is admired globally for its symmetry, elegance, and attention to intricate detail. The beauty of Mughal architecture is unparalleled in its grandeur, with its signature domes, minarets, gardens, and intricate stone carvings. The Mughals not only built majestic structures but also set the tone for artistic expression in India for centuries, leaving behind a legacy of architectural brilliance that continues to inspire admiration and awe.

One of the most remarkable aspects of Mughal architecture is its use of symmetry and balance. Whether it was a tomb, mosque, palace, or fort, symmetry was a fundamental principle in Mughal designs. The architects of the Mughal era were meticulous in creating layouts that emphasized harmony and proportion. Structures were built on axial plans, with central domes or minarets serving as focal points around which the rest of the building was aligned. This sense of balance was not only limited to individual buildings but extended to entire complexes, where gardens, courtyards, fountains, and pavilions were arranged with geometric precision. The emphasis on symmetry reflected the Mughals' desire to create a sense of order and serenity, which they associated with paradise as described in Islamic tradition. This concept is particularly evident in the layout of Mughal gardens, known as charbagh, which were divided into four quadrants symbolizing the Islamic ideal of heaven.

The use of materials in Mughal architecture also played a significant role in its beauty. The Mughals were masters in using high-quality materials such as red sandstone, white marble, semi-precious stones, and in some cases, even gold and silver to embellish their buildings. Red sandstone, quarried from places like Fatehpur Sikri and Agra, was often used for large public buildings, forts, and palaces. Its warm hue gave these structures a majestic and imposing appearance, while intricate carvings on its surface added an element of delicacy to the otherwise robust facades. The Taj Mahal, built by Shah Jahan, is an exquisite example of the Mughal mastery of white marble. This pure, luminous material was used to create a building that appears ethereal, especially when its surface reflects the changing colors of the sky at different times of the day. The marble in the Taj Mahal is inlaid with intricate floral patterns made from precious and semi-precious stones such as jasper, jade, turquoise, and lapis lazuli, creating a delicate interplay of colors against the white stone. This technique, known as pietra dura, became a hallmark of Mughal decorative art and added a unique layer of visual interest to the architecture.

Domes are perhaps the most recognizable feature of Mughal architecture, symbolizing grandeur and heavenly aspirations. Inspired by Persian and Islamic architectural traditions, the Mughals perfected the art of constructing large, bulbous domes that seem to float above the structures. These domes often crown the central buildings, serving as both aesthetic and structural marvels. The sheer size and scale of these domes, coupled with their flawless symmetry and proportion, created a sense of awe for viewers. The Taj Mahal's iconic central dome is a masterpiece of Mughal engineering, rising majestically above the building and visible from miles away. These domes were often accompanied by smaller domes or chattris (domed pavilions), further adding to the architectural complexity and beauty of the structures.

The interiors of these domes were often decorated with intricate patterns and calligraphy, creating a celestial atmosphere within.

Minarets, another hallmark of Mughal architecture, were typically tall, slender towers that flanked the main building, particularly in mosques and monumental tombs. These minarets were not only functional, serving as places from which the call to prayer was given, but also symbolic, representing a connection between the heavens and the earth. Their slender, elegant form added verticality to the otherwise horizontal layout of Mughal buildings, creating a sense of balance and grace. The Taj Mahal, for instance, is surrounded by four towering minarets, each of which enhances the overall symmetry of the complex while providing a sense of elevation to the mausoleum.

Another key element of Mughal architecture is the extensive use of calligraphy and geometric patterns. Islamic art traditionally avoids depicting living beings, so Mughal architects and artists developed a sophisticated visual language based on intricate calligraphy, geometric designs, and floral motifs. Quranic verses, often written in beautiful, flowing Arabic script, were inscribed on the surfaces of buildings, particularly around entrances and on domes. These inscriptions were not merely decorative; they also conveyed religious and philosophical messages, invoking blessings, protection, and divine favor. Geometric patterns, on the other hand, were used to symbolize the infinite nature of creation and the order of the universe. These patterns were meticulously crafted, with each line and shape calculated to fit perfectly within the overall design. Mughal artisans used materials like marble and sandstone to create these intricate patterns, often inlaid into the walls of buildings. The combination of calligraphy and geometric design gave Mughal buildings a sense of intellectual depth and spiritual resonance, elevating them from mere architectural feats to deeply meaningful spaces.

One of the remarkable contributions of Mughal architecture to world heritage is the innovation of large-scale gardens, often referred to as "paradise gardens." Mughal emperors had a deep appreciation for nature, and they sought to integrate it into their architectural masterpieces. Mughal gardens, designed in the charbagh style, were typically divided into four sections by water channels and pathways, with fountains and trees placed at symmetrical intervals. These gardens were not just ornamental but also represented an earthly paradise, a reflection of the Islamic concept of Jannat (heaven). The Mughals' careful cultivation of trees, flowers, and water features enhanced the sensory experience of their palaces and tombs. The gardens around the Taj Mahal are a stunning example of this concept, with their lush greenery, flowing fountains, and serene atmosphere creating a tranquil space that complements the elegance of the marble mausoleum.

The forts and palaces built during the Mughal era are further examples of the empire's architectural brilliance. The Agra Fort, for instance, is a massive complex built primarily of red sandstone and later expanded with marble. It served as the residence of the Mughal emperors for generations and housed numerous palaces, audience halls, and gardens within its walls. The fort's design combines military strength with aesthetic elegance, featuring intricate carvings, delicate latticework, and impressive gates. Similarly, the Red Fort in Delhi, another of Shah Jahan's masterpieces, is an imposing structure that showcases the Mughals' skill in fortification while also serving as a symbol of imperial power and splendor. The fort's massive walls are contrasted by the exquisite decoration of the buildings inside, including the Diwan-i-Aam (Hall of Public Audience) and the Diwan-i-Khas (Hall of Private Audience), where the emperor held court.

Mughal mosques are equally renowned for their beauty and grandeur. One of the most significant examples is the Jama Masjid in Delhi, commissioned by Shah Jahan. This mosque is one of the largest in India and a stunning example of Mughal architecture. It features three grand gates, four towers, and two minarets constructed of strips of red sandstone and white marble. The mosque's prayer hall is covered by three domes, with the central dome being the largest, and it opens onto a vast courtyard that can hold thousands of worshippers. The scale, symmetry, and detailed ornamentation of the mosque make it a monumental example of Mughal religious architecture.

In addition to these grand monuments, the Mughals also built smaller but equally intricate buildings such as tombs and pavilions. Humayun's Tomb in Delhi, built in the mid-16th century, is considered one of the earliest examples of Mughal architecture and served as a precursor to the later development of monumental Mughal tombs, including the Taj Mahal. It features a combination of red sandstone and white marble, along with a charbagh garden layout, which became a standard feature of later Mughal tombs. Similarly, Itmad-ud-Daulah's Tomb, often referred to as the "Baby Taj," is a beautiful marble mausoleum that predates the Taj Mahal and displays some of the techniques, such as pietra dura, that would later be perfected in the construction of the Taj.

One cannot discuss the beauty of Mughal architecture without acknowledging its cultural significance. Mughal buildings were not only physical structures but also symbols of power, faith, and identity. The Mughals, as rulers of a vast and diverse empire, used architecture as a means of expressing their dominance, their spiritual devotion, and their unique blend of cultural influences. Each building, from the massive forts to the intricate tombs, was a statement of the emperor's vision and authority. At the same time, the beauty and refinement of these buildings reflected the Mughals' love for art and their desire to create a lasting legacy. Today, these monuments stand as a testament to the cultural richness of the Mughal era and continue to draw millions of visitors from around the world who come to admire their timeless beauty.

Chapter 5: Why the Taj Mahal Changes Color

The Taj Mahal, one of the world's most iconic monuments, is renowned not only for its architectural beauty but also for the way it seems to change color throughout the day. This mesmerizing characteristic has fascinated visitors and scholars for centuries, adding an almost magical quality to the monument's already stunning presence. The way the Taj Mahal transforms from dawn to dusk, and even in the moonlight, has been described as one of the most enchanting phenomena in the world of architecture. The color changes are primarily due to the interplay of natural light with the materials used in its construction, particularly the white marble, and the varying atmospheric conditions. However, this effect is more than just a visual trick; it has deep symbolic meanings, reflecting different moods and emotions that align with the monument's essence as a tribute to love and loss.

The Taj Mahal is constructed primarily from white marble, a material that has unique reflective and refractive properties. White marble, especially the kind used in the Taj Mahal, has a translucency that allows it to absorb and reflect light in different ways depending on the time of day and the quality of light in the atmosphere. This characteristic gives the Taj Mahal its ability to change color. In the early morning, as the first rays of the sun strike the monument, the marble takes on a soft, golden-pink hue, as though it is gently waking up with the day. This effect is caused by the low angle of the sun and the warm tones of the early sunlight. The delicate pinks and golds that appear at this time of day create a feeling of tranquility and calm, often interpreted as symbolizing the hope and promise of a new day, just as Shah Jahan hoped for an eternal union with his beloved wife, Mumtaz Mahal.

As the sun rises higher in the sky and the day becomes brighter, the Taj Mahal undergoes a noticeable transformation. By late morning and noon, the sunlight becomes more direct and intense, causing the marble to appear pure white. The bright white marble at midday is perhaps the Taj Mahal's most iconic look, and it is during this time that the monument stands in its full glory, bathed in the brilliance of the sun. The intense white reflects the powerful midday sun, making the Taj Mahal appear almost blindingly bright and giving it a sense of majesty and dominance. The monument's pristine white appearance at this time of day can be seen as symbolizing purity, eternal love, and the unblemished beauty of Mumtaz Mahal, whom Shah Jahan wished to immortalize in this flawless form. The midday sun also enhances the symmetrical perfection of the structure, as every detail of the intricate carvings and inlaid stonework becomes more visible and distinct under the clear, bright light.

As the afternoon progresses and the sun begins its descent, the Taj Mahal's appearance shifts once again. The harsh midday light softens, and the marble takes on a more golden hue as the sun lowers in the sky. The warmer tones of the late afternoon light create a sense of serenity and reflection, as though the monument is preparing for the close of the day. The golden glow of the marble at this time of day is often interpreted as a reflection of the setting sun, symbolizing the inevitable passage of time and the fading of life's moments. For many, this transformation evokes a sense of melancholy and introspection, as the golden tones remind them of the love between Shah Jahan and Mumtaz Mahal that, though eternal, was also tinged with sorrow and loss. The late afternoon Taj Mahal exudes a peaceful, almost contemplative atmosphere, encouraging visitors to reflect on the nature of love, memory, and impermanence.

One of the most captivating transformations of the Taj Mahal occurs during sunset. As the sun sets, the colors of the sky change from gold to orange, pink, and finally deep purple and blue. These changing colors are reflected on the surface of the Taj Mahal, creating a breathtaking display of shifting hues. The marble seems to absorb the colors of the sky, creating a mesmerizing spectacle that leaves onlookers spellbound. As the day ends, the Taj Mahal often takes on a soft, rosy glow, as if it is bathed in the light of a fading sunset. This soft pinkish hue is seen by many as a symbol of love's tenderness and the enduring beauty of romantic devotion. The twilight hues also impart a sense of calmness and peacefulness to the monument, reinforcing the idea that the Taj Mahal is not only a symbol of eternal love but also of the peace that comes with acceptance of life's cycles.

One of the most magical aspects of the Taj Mahal's color-changing phenomenon is its appearance under moonlight. On nights when the full moon is shining brightly, the Taj Mahal takes on an otherworldly glow. The white marble, which reflects sunlight so brilliantly during the day, also reflects the cooler, softer light of the moon, creating a silvery sheen that makes the monument appear ethereal and almost ghostly. Under the full moon, the Taj Mahal seems to glow from within, as though it is illuminated by some inner light. This silvery glow enhances the monument's mystical and romantic aura, making it a favorite time for couples and visitors to experience the Taj Mahal. The moonlit Taj Mahal, with its shimmering, almost translucent appearance, is often described as a dreamlike vision, a reflection of the celestial and divine love that Shah Jahan envisioned when he built the monument for his beloved wife. The moonlight adds a layer of magic and mystery to the Taj Mahal, creating a sense of timelessness and spiritual transcendence that transcends the earthly realm.

The changing colors of the Taj Mahal are also influenced by the weather and atmospheric conditions. On clear, sunny days, the monument's color transitions are more distinct, with the shifts from pink to white to gold being more pronounced. However, on cloudy or rainy days, the Taj Mahal takes on a more subdued appearance. The marble appears more gray or even blue, as it reflects the overcast sky.

This muted appearance, though less dramatic than the vibrant colors seen on sunny days, imparts a sense of quiet dignity and solemnity to the monument. The Taj Mahal in the rain or under cloudy skies evokes feelings of introspection and a deeper connection to the emotions of loss and longing that inspired its creation. The grayish tones can be seen as representing the sorrow and grief that Shah Jahan felt after the death of Mumtaz Mahal, adding another layer of emotional depth to the monument's already profound symbolism.

In addition to the light and atmospheric conditions, the intricate craftsmanship of the Taj Mahal also plays a role in its changing appearance. The monument is adorned with delicate carvings, floral motifs, and inlaid semi-precious stones, all of which catch the light in different ways depending on the time of day and the angle of the sun. The pietra dura inlay work, which features precious stones like jasper, jade, turquoise, and lapis lazuli, reflects light differently depending on the colors and qualities of the stones. As the light changes throughout the day, the inlaid stones seem to shimmer and change color, adding to the overall effect of the monument's transformation. The marble itself is also carved with intricate patterns, and the way the light hits these carvings at different angles creates shadows and highlights that enhance the monument's sense of depth and complexity. This attention to detail is a testament to the skill and artistry of the craftsmen who built the Taj Mahal and adds to the monument's enduring beauty and fascination.

Symbolism plays a significant role in understanding why the Taj Mahal changes color. Shah Jahan, who commissioned the Taj Mahal as a tomb for his beloved wife Mumtaz Mahal, intended the monument to be a symbol of their eternal love. The changing colors of the Taj Mahal reflect the many facets of love—its beauty, its sorrow, its joy, and its tranquility. Each phase of the day represents a different aspect of the love story between Shah Jahan and Mumtaz Mahal, from the pinks of dawn symbolizing new beginnings, to the bright white of midday representing the purity of their love, to the golden hues of sunset reflecting the passage of time and the inevitable end of life. The moonlit Taj Mahal, with its ethereal glow, represents the eternal and transcendent nature of their love, which, like the monument itself, will endure for all time. The changing colors also reflect the emotions of loss and longing that Shah Jahan experienced after Mumtaz Mahal's death, with the monument serving as both a tribute to her memory and a testament to the power of love to transcend the boundaries of life and death.

In conclusion, the Taj Mahal's ability to change color throughout the day is one of the many reasons why it is considered one of the most beautiful and iconic structures in the world. This color-changing phenomenon, caused by the interaction of light with the white marble and the atmospheric conditions, adds a dynamic and almost magical quality to the monument. The changing colors not only enhance the visual beauty of the Taj Mahal but also serve as a powerful symbol of the love, loss, and eternal devotion that inspired its creation. Whether viewed at dawn, in the bright light of midday, at sunset, or under the soft glow of the moon, the Taj Mahal continues to captivate and inspire awe, standing as a timeless testament to the enduring power of love.

Chapter 6: The Gardens Surrounding the Taj Mahal

The gardens surrounding the Taj Mahal are an integral part of its majestic beauty and play a significant role in enhancing the overall aesthetic experience of the monument. Known as the Charbagh or Mughal garden, this vast, meticulously designed area offers an oasis of serenity that contrasts with the grand architectural splendor of the mausoleum itself. The Charbagh is laid out in a symmetrical, geometric pattern, following the traditional Persian garden design principles that emphasize harmony and balance. This particular garden style was introduced to India by the Mughal emperors, and the Taj Mahal's garden is one of the finest examples of this fusion of Persian and Indian landscaping traditions.

As one approaches the Taj Mahal, the first thing that strikes the eye is the long, straight path leading up to the white marble mausoleum. This path is flanked by lush green lawns, perfectly manicured to maintain a consistent appearance throughout the year. Dividing the gardens into four equal parts, a wide water channel runs down the middle, creating a stunning reflection of the Taj Mahal, which gives the illusion of the monument floating ethereally on the water. This channel, known as the 'Nahar,' is lined with small fountains that gently spout water, adding to the sense of tranquility that permeates the entire space. The water used for the channel and the fountains was traditionally supplied through an intricate system of aqueducts and underground reservoirs, showcasing the Mughal engineers' advanced understanding of hydraulics.

The garden itself is divided into four quadrants, in accordance with the Charbagh style, symbolizing the four gardens of paradise described in Islamic texts. This design holds deep spiritual significance, as paradise in Islamic culture is often envisioned as a lush, verdant garden with flowing rivers and abundant shade. The choice to structure the garden around this concept emphasizes the Taj Mahal's role as a monument to eternal love, transcending earthly existence to reach a heavenly state. In the context of the Taj Mahal, the gardens not only serve as a physical space of beauty but also as a metaphorical representation of paradise, a place where Shah Jahan's love for Mumtaz Mahal can endure for eternity.

A key feature of the garden's design is its precise symmetry. Each of the four quadrants is further divided into smaller sections by pathways, which intersect at right angles, creating a grid-like layout. These pathways, made of red sandstone, contrast beautifully with the green grass and the white marble of the Taj Mahal, creating a visual harmony that is pleasing to the eye. Along the edges of these pathways, there are numerous flower beds, which during the Mughal era would have been filled with an assortment of fragrant flowers and medicinal herbs. The vibrant colors of the flowers, ranging from reds and yellows to pinks and purples, would have added an additional layer of beauty to the garden, further enhancing the sensory experience for visitors. Though some of the original plant species may have changed over time, efforts have been made to preserve the garden's historical authenticity by maintaining similar floral arrangements.

The trees planted in the garden also serve a dual purpose, both aesthetic and practical. Tall cypress trees, known for their conical shapes, line the pathways and symbolize death, while the fruit-bearing trees, such as pomegranates and oranges, represent life and regeneration. This juxtaposition of life and death is a poignant reminder of the themes that the Taj Mahal embodies: love, loss, and the hope for eternal reunion in the afterlife. The cypress trees, with their dark green foliage, stand in sharp contrast to the brightness of the surrounding landscape, adding a sense of gravitas to the otherwise peaceful ambiance of the garden.

In addition to the trees and flowers, there are several small pavilions and gazebos scattered throughout the garden, which would have provided shaded areas for visitors to rest and enjoy the cool breeze coming off the Yamuna River, which runs adjacent to the Taj Mahal. These structures, though modest in comparison to the grandeur of the Taj Mahal, are finely crafted and blend seamlessly into the overall design of the garden. Built from the same red sandstone used in other Mughal architectural projects, these pavilions echo the larger structures within the Taj Mahal complex, further contributing to the sense of unity and cohesion in the overall design.

One of the most remarkable aspects of the garden is how it changes throughout the day and across different seasons. In the early morning, as the sun rises, the garden is bathed in a soft, golden light that gives the entire area a dreamlike quality. The reflection of the Taj Mahal in the central water channel appears even more striking at this time, as the stillness of the water mirrors the monument's form with almost perfect clarity. As the day progresses and the sun climbs higher, the colors of the garden become more vibrant, and the interplay of light and shadow creates constantly shifting patterns on the grass, trees, and pathways. During the hot summer months, the garden provides a cool refuge, as the shade from the trees and the water from the fountains create a refreshing environment for visitors. In the cooler winter months, the garden takes on a more subdued tone, with the mist rising from the river in the early mornings, giving the entire space a mystical, almost otherworldly atmosphere.

The gardens surrounding the Taj Mahal are not just an afterthought to the grand monument but are an essential part of the overall experience. They reflect the Mughals' deep appreciation for nature and their understanding of the profound connection between the natural and spiritual worlds. The meticulous planning and execution of the garden design show that it was intended to complement the Taj Mahal, both visually and symbolically. Every element, from the symmetrical layout to the choice of plants and trees, has been carefully considered to create a space that evokes a sense of peace, harmony, and transcendence. For visitors, the gardens offer a chance to reflect on the deeper meanings of love, loss, and the eternal, while also providing a place of beauty and serenity that enhances the magnificence of the Taj Mahal itself.

The integration of water, greenery, and stone in the garden mirrors the elements of the Taj Mahal's architecture, creating a seamless transition between the natural and man-made worlds. The garden's design encourages visitors to not only admire the Taj Mahal from a distance but to walk through the pathways, sit by the fountains, and experience the tranquility of the space. This interaction with the garden allows for a deeper appreciation of the monument, as one becomes enveloped in the peaceful atmosphere that surrounds it. The gentle sound of flowing water, the soft rustling of leaves in the breeze, and the fragrance of flowers all contribute to a multisensory experience that leaves a lasting impression on those who visit this world-renowned site.

Chapter 7: Exploring the Inside of the Taj Mahal

Exploring the inside of the Taj Mahal is an awe-inspiring experience, one that reveals a level of craftsmanship and artistry that few structures in the world can match. The moment you step inside, you are transported into a realm of breathtaking beauty and profound emotion, as every detail within the walls of the mausoleum has been designed with precision and care to honor the memory of Mumtaz Mahal, the beloved wife of Emperor Shah Jahan. The interior space, though modest in comparison to the sprawling gardens and the grand exterior, is imbued with a sense of reverence and solemnity that makes it feel almost like stepping into a sacred temple. The atmosphere is hushed, with visitors often speaking in whispers as they take in the stunning details that cover every inch of the interior.

The central chamber of the Taj Mahal is perhaps the most significant part of the structure, as it houses the false tombs of Mumtaz Mahal and Shah Jahan. These cenotaphs are not their actual resting places, as the real tombs lie beneath the main chamber in a crypt that is not open to the public. Nevertheless, the cenotaphs are elaborately decorated and serve as symbolic representations of the emperor and his queen. Crafted from the same flawless white marble that makes up the rest of the Taj Mahal, the cenotaphs are adorned with intricate inlays of precious and semi-precious stones, including jade, lapis lazuli, and turquoise. These inlays form delicate floral patterns, with each flower and vine carefully positioned to create a sense of harmony and elegance. The craftsmanship involved in creating these inlays is remarkable, as artisans had to meticulously carve tiny grooves into the marble to fit each stone perfectly, a process that required both immense skill and patience.

The cenotaph of Mumtaz Mahal is slightly larger than that of Shah Jahan, a subtle but poignant reminder that this mausoleum was originally built for her. Both cenotaphs are inscribed with verses from the Quran, written in delicate calligraphy that wraps around the edges of the tombs like a ribbon. These inscriptions not only add to the beauty of the cenotaphs but also serve a spiritual purpose, invoking blessings for the souls of the departed. The use of calligraphy throughout the interior of the Taj Mahal is one of its most striking features, and the verses are chosen carefully to reflect themes of paradise, eternal love, and divine mercy. The words are not merely decorative but are intended to guide visitors in reflecting on the deeper meaning of life, death, and the afterlife.

One of the most impressive aspects of the Taj Mahal's interior is the dome that rises above the central chamber. This massive, soaring dome is a masterpiece of Mughal engineering, and its shape is designed to create a sense of both grandeur and intimacy. As you look up, the dome seems to float effortlessly above you, its smooth, curved surface catching the light that filters in through the small, latticework windows. The dome is designed with perfect symmetry, and its interior is decorated with a series of geometric patterns that further enhance its ethereal quality. The acoustics of the chamber beneath the dome are also carefully considered, and even the softest sounds echo gently, creating a sense of calm and stillness that adds to the solemn atmosphere of the space.

Surrounding the central chamber are four smaller, octagonal chambers, each connected to the central space by arched doorways. These chambers are also constructed from white marble and feature similar inlays of precious stones and calligraphic inscriptions. In the past, these chambers may have served as places for visitors to meditate, pray, or reflect on the lives of Mumtaz Mahal and Shah Jahan. The symmetry of the Taj Mahal's design extends to these chambers, with each one mirroring the others in layout and decoration. This balance and harmony are central to the Mughal architectural style, as they reflect the order and perfection of the universe, concepts that were deeply important in Islamic thought.

Another feature of the interior that captivates visitors is the intricate jali screens, which are made of intricately carved marble latticework. These screens, which surround the cenotaphs, were designed to allow light and air to flow into the space while also maintaining a sense of privacy and seclusion. The patterns on the jali screens are incredibly complex, featuring geometric shapes and floral motifs that appear delicate despite being carved from solid marble. The light that filters through these screens creates beautiful patterns on the marble floor, further adding to the sense of tranquility and spirituality within the chamber. The interplay of light and shadow is a recurring theme throughout the Taj Mahal, and nowhere is it more evident than in these jali screens, where the dappled sunlight seems to dance on the surfaces, giving the space an almost mystical quality.

The floor of the Taj Mahal's interior is another marvel of design, crafted from a combination of white and black marble that forms intricate geometric patterns. These patterns, much like the inlays on the walls and the jali screens, are carefully arranged to create a sense of symmetry and balance. The black marble outlines serve as a striking contrast to the gleaming white marble, drawing attention to the precision of the design. Each tile is laid with meticulous care, contributing to the overall sense of perfection that permeates every corner of the Taj Mahal.

One of the unique aspects of exploring the interior of the Taj Mahal is the way in which light is used to enhance the beauty of the space. The natural light that filters in through the jali screens and the small windows in the dome is soft and diffuse, creating an atmosphere that is both peaceful and ethereal. This play of light and shadow is complemented by the way the marble itself seems to glow in certain conditions. The white marble of the Taj Mahal has a unique quality in that it changes color depending on the time of day and the weather. In the early morning, the marble takes on a soft pink hue, while at midday it gleams a bright, pure white. As the sun sets, the marble reflects the warm golden light of the evening, and under the moonlight, it appears almost silver, giving the Taj Mahal a magical, otherworldly quality. This shifting palette of colors adds to the sense of wonder that visitors feel as they move through the interior, as the monument seems to be constantly changing and evolving before their eyes.

In addition to the beauty of the structure itself, the interior of the Taj Mahal also holds a deep emotional significance. For many visitors, standing in the central chamber is a profoundly moving experience, as the space is imbued with the story of Shah Jahan's enduring love for Mumtaz Mahal. The quiet, reverent atmosphere of the interior encourages reflection on the themes of love, loss, and the passage of time. The fact that Shah Jahan himself was later interred in the Taj Mahal alongside Mumtaz Mahal adds an additional layer of poignancy to the experience, as visitors are reminded of the emperor's deep devotion to his wife and the lengths he went to in order to honor her memory. The interior of the Taj Mahal is not just a beautiful space but a place that invites visitors to connect with the emotions that inspired its creation, making it one of the most powerful monuments to love in the world.

Exploring the inside of the Taj Mahal is an experience that stays with visitors long after they leave. The combination of exquisite craftsmanship, intricate detail, and profound symbolism creates a space that feels timeless and transcendent. Whether it is the delicate inlays of precious stones, the soaring dome, the intricate jali screens, or the cenotaphs themselves, every element of the interior has been carefully designed to evoke a sense of peace, beauty, and reverence. The Taj Mahal's interior is not only a testament to the incredible skill of the artisans who built it but also a reminder of the powerful emotions that drove its creation. For those who visit, stepping inside the Taj Mahal is not just an exploration of a physical space but a journey into the heart of one of the greatest love stories ever told.

Chapter 8: The Minarets of the Taj Mahal

The minarets of the Taj Mahal are one of the most striking features of this world-renowned monument, standing tall and gracefully at each of the four corners of the platform on which the mausoleum is built. These towering structures are not only a key component of the overall architectural design of the Taj Mahal but also serve both symbolic and practical purposes. Rising to a height of approximately 40 meters (131 feet), the minarets play an essential role in creating the balance and symmetry that characterize the Mughal architecture of the Taj Mahal. Each of the four minarets was meticulously constructed to ensure perfect alignment with the central structure, contributing to the monument's sense of harmony and visual perfection.

From a distance, the minarets seem to soar effortlessly into the sky, their slender, cylindrical forms tapering gradually as they rise. The white marble used in their construction mirrors the material of the main mausoleum, ensuring a seamless visual connection between the minarets and the central structure. Despite their impressive height, the minarets do not overshadow the Taj Mahal but rather enhance its beauty by framing it on all sides, creating a sense of grandeur and scale. This framing effect is particularly noticeable when viewed from afar, as the four minarets seem to stand guard around the mausoleum, giving it an air of regality and solemnity.

One of the most interesting aspects of the minarets is their slightly outward-leaning design, a subtle but significant feature that reflects the advanced engineering skills of the architects and builders of the Taj Mahal. This outward tilt is not immediately noticeable to the casual observer, but it was intentionally incorporated into the design to protect the central structure in the event of an earthquake. Should a natural disaster occur, the minarets would collapse away from the main mausoleum rather than toward it, thereby preventing any damage to the tomb of Mumtaz Mahal and Shah Jahan. This ingenious design demonstrates the foresight of the Mughal architects and engineers, who not only focused on aesthetics but also took into account the structural integrity of the monument for generations to come.

The design and construction of the minarets also hold deep symbolic meaning. In traditional Islamic architecture, minarets are commonly associated with mosques, where they are used to call the faithful to prayer. While the Taj Mahal is a mausoleum rather than a mosque, the inclusion of minarets reflects its connection to Islamic traditions and serves as a reminder of the religious significance of the monument. The Taj Mahal was built in a deeply spiritual context, and the minarets, with their towering presence, symbolize the ascent to the heavens and the eternal nature of love and devotion. Their placement at the four corners of the platform further emphasizes the concept of balance and order, themes that are central to both Islamic architecture and the overall design of the Taj Mahal.

At the base of each minaret is an octagonal platform, also made of white marble, which provides a stable foundation for the towering structure. The platform is intricately decorated with floral and geometric patterns, reflecting the Mughal attention to detail and their love for combining beauty with function. Visitors approaching the Taj Mahal from the main entrance are immediately drawn to these platforms, as they form a key part of the visual approach to the monument. The platforms also serve a practical purpose, as they provide additional stability to the minarets, ensuring that the tall structures remain secure even in the face of environmental stresses such as wind and weather.

The cylindrical shafts of the minarets are divided into three sections, each marked by a balcony that encircles the tower. These balconies are supported by delicate stone brackets, which are not only functional but also add an element of decorative finesse to the overall design. The stonework in these brackets is incredibly intricate, with floral motifs and geometric patterns carved with great precision. These balconies provide a visual break in the smooth vertical lines of the minarets, creating a rhythmic pattern that draws the eye upward toward the sky. The progression from the wide base to the slender, tapering top of the minarets is a masterpiece of proportion, as the architects managed to create a sense of both strength and lightness in the same structure.

At the very top of each minaret is a small domed pavilion, known as a chhatri, which is another hallmark of Mughal architecture. These chhatris are exquisitely designed, featuring intricate stone carvings and delicate latticework. The domes are topped with a gilded finial, adding a touch of grandeur to the otherwise understated elegance of the minarets. The chhatris not only serve as a decorative element but also have a practical function, as they provide shade and protection for those who may have once ascended the minarets. In the past, these minarets were accessible to visitors and may have been used as observation towers, offering panoramic views of the Taj Mahal complex and the surrounding landscape, including the Yamuna River. Standing at the top of one of these minarets, one could take in the full majesty of the Taj Mahal and the surrounding Charbagh garden, an experience that must have been truly breathtaking.

The minarets are also adorned with intricate calligraphic inscriptions, much like the rest of the Taj Mahal. These inscriptions, which consist of verses from the Quran, are carefully chosen to reflect the themes of paradise, love, and eternal peace. The calligraphy is rendered in black stone, providing a striking contrast to the gleaming white marble of the minarets. The script itself is a fine example of Mughal calligraphy, known for its elegance and fluidity. The inscriptions are not just decorative but also serve a spiritual purpose, reminding visitors of the sacred nature of the Taj Mahal and the eternal bond between Shah Jahan and Mumtaz Mahal. The verses selected for the minarets were chosen with great care, ensuring that they aligned with the overall themes of the monument and contributed to the meditative atmosphere of the space.

In addition to their architectural and symbolic significance, the minarets of the Taj Mahal also serve a functional purpose in the overall design of the complex. Their placement at the four corners of the platform creates a sense of enclosure around the central mausoleum, giving the entire structure a feeling of protection and completeness. The minarets help to define the space of the Taj Mahal, framing the mausoleum and drawing the eye toward its central dome. This framing effect is particularly noticeable when viewed from the main entrance gate, as the minarets create a visual pathway that guides visitors' attention toward the main structure. The symmetry and balance created by the minarets are key to the overall aesthetic impact of the Taj Mahal, as they ensure that the monument is seen as a unified whole rather than a collection of individual parts.

At different times of the day, the minarets take on different appearances depending on the quality of light. In the soft glow of the early morning, they seem to shimmer with a pale pink hue, while in the bright midday sun, they stand in stark, gleaming contrast against the deep blue sky. As the sun sets, the minarets take on a warm, golden tone, and under the light of the moon, they appear almost ethereal, blending into the silvery-white marble of the mausoleum. This changing play of light and shadow throughout the day enhances the sense of timelessness that surrounds the Taj Mahal, making it feel as though the monument is constantly shifting and evolving, much like the love story that inspired its creation.

For many visitors, the minarets are a symbol of the enduring legacy of the Mughal Empire and its contributions to the art of architecture. The Taj Mahal, with its perfect proportions, intricate details, and deep symbolism, represents the pinnacle of Mughal architectural achievement, and the minarets are a key part of what makes this monument so iconic. Their presence not only adds to the visual grandeur of the Taj Mahal but also reminds visitors of the deep spiritual and emotional significance of the structure. As one walks around the Taj Mahal, the minarets serve as constant companions, framing each view and adding depth and perspective to the overall experience.

Exploring the minarets of the Taj Mahal, whether by observing their intricate details up close or by appreciating their graceful silhouettes from a distance, is a reminder of the incredible skill and artistry that went into the creation of this monument. They stand as a testament to the genius of the architects, the dedication of the craftsmen, and the profound love that inspired Shah Jahan to build one of the most beautiful structures in the world. The minarets are not just architectural elements; they are integral to the story of the Taj Mahal, a story that continues to captivate and inspire people from all over the world.

Chapter 9: Myths and Legends of the Taj Mahal

The Taj Mahal, one of the most iconic structures in the world, has not only captured the imagination of architects, historians, and travelers but also become the subject of numerous myths and legends that have swirled around its ethereal beauty for centuries. As a symbol of eternal love and architectural brilliance, it has naturally inspired tales that range from the romantic and mystical to the dark and fantastical. These stories, although not based in historical fact, have become deeply intertwined with the monument's legacy, contributing to the allure and mystery that surrounds this magnificent structure. Exploring the myths and legends of the Taj Mahal offers a fascinating glimpse into how folklore, cultural narratives, and historical interpretations evolve around such a monumental structure.

One of the most famous myths about the Taj Mahal is that it was intended to have a counterpart—a "Black Taj Mahal"—that Shah Jahan planned to build across the Yamuna River. According to legend, Shah Jahan, after completing the white marble Taj Mahal as a mausoleum for his beloved wife Mumtaz Mahal, wished to construct an identical but black-colored version for himself on the opposite bank of the river. The two structures, it is said, would have mirrored each other perfectly, symbolizing the balance between life and death, day and night, and love and mourning. The myth further claims that the two Taj Mahals would have been connected by a bridge spanning the Yamuna, creating a majestic and eternal bond between the emperor and his queen. However, the Black Taj Mahal was never built, according to the story, because Shah Jahan was overthrown by his son Aurangzeb before the construction could begin. While this tale has captivated many, there is no historical or archaeological evidence to support the existence of such a plan. Some scholars believe the myth may have originated from the dark reflections of the white Taj Mahal seen in the Yamuna River's waters at night, giving the illusion of a black monument.

Another popular legend revolves around the supposed cruelty of Shah Jahan toward the artisans and craftsmen who worked on the Taj Mahal. It is often said that after the completion of the monument, Shah Jahan ordered that the hands of the artisans be severed or their eyes gouged out to ensure that they could never replicate the beauty of the Taj Mahal. This grim tale paints Shah Jahan as a ruler so obsessed with the uniqueness and perfection of the Taj Mahal that he was willing to commit terrible acts to preserve its singularity. Despite the enduring popularity of this story, historians have found no credible evidence to support it. In fact, Shah Jahan was known to be a patron of the arts and architecture, and it seems unlikely that he would have taken such drastic measures against the very people who had brought his vision to life. The legend, however, continues to be retold, possibly because it adds a darker, more dramatic layer to the otherwise romantic image of the Taj Mahal.

The legend of the Taj Mahal also extends into the realm of the supernatural. Some stories suggest that the site of the Taj Mahal was haunted long before the construction of the mausoleum began. According to one myth, the land on which the Taj Mahal stands was originally the site of a Hindu temple dedicated to Lord Shiva. This temple, known as "Tejo Mahalaya," was allegedly demolished by Shah Jahan to make way for the Taj Mahal, and the spirits of the temple's deities are said to haunt the site to this day. This particular legend has been propagated by certain factions who argue that the Taj Mahal was not originally an Islamic structure but was instead appropriated from Hindu culture. However, mainstream historians and archaeologists have consistently debunked this claim, citing ample historical records and documentation that point to the Taj Mahal being an original Mughal construction. Nevertheless, the myth persists, fueled by a desire to reclaim historical narratives and reinterpret the past.

There are also myths surrounding the mysterious symbolism hidden within the design and architecture of the Taj Mahal. Some believe that the structure was designed with secret codes and hidden messages embedded in its intricate patterns, calligraphy, and geometric designs. These supposed codes are thought to reveal esoteric truths about the nature of life, death, and the universe. While it is true that the Taj Mahal is rich in symbolic meaning—especially in its use of Islamic motifs such as the Quranic inscriptions and the garden's symbolic representation of paradise—there is no historical evidence to suggest that the monument contains hidden codes or messages. The precision and complexity of the design are a testament to the skill of the Mughal architects and artisans, but the idea of secret messages remains firmly in the realm of myth and speculation.

The romantic legend of how Shah Jahan and Mumtaz Mahal fell in love has also been mythologized over time, with some versions of the story taking on almost fairy-tale qualities. According to one popular version, Shah Jahan, then Prince Khurram, first met Mumtaz Mahal at a bazaar, where she was selling silk and glass beads. Struck by her beauty, intelligence, and grace, he immediately fell in love with her and vowed to make her his queen. In this version of the story, their love is portrayed as instant and pure, a bond forged by fate. While it is true that Shah Jahan and Mumtaz Mahal shared a deep and enduring love, the story of their meeting in a bazaar is likely a romantic embellishment. Historical records suggest that their marriage was arranged by their families, as was common among royalty at the time. Nonetheless, the story of their love has taken on a life of its own, evolving into a mythic tale that reinforces the narrative of the Taj Mahal as the ultimate symbol of eternal love.

One of the more outlandish myths about the Taj Mahal involves the claim that it was built by extraterrestrials or advanced ancient civilizations. This theory, while widely dismissed by historians and archaeologists, has found a niche following among those who believe in ancient astronaut theories. Proponents of this myth argue that the precision and complexity of the Taj Mahal's design, particularly its perfectly symmetrical layout and the intricacies of its inlay work, are beyond the capabilities of the Mughal-era artisans and must have been the work of advanced beings. They point to the alignment of the monument with certain celestial bodies and the use of materials that were transported from distant locations as evidence of otherworldly involvement. While these claims are based on conjecture rather than fact, they reflect a broader fascination with the mystery and beauty of the Taj Mahal and its ability to inspire awe and wonder across cultures and time periods.

Another persistent legend is that Shah Jahan intended the Taj Mahal to be a symbol not just of his love for Mumtaz Mahal but also of the Mughal Empire's dominance and power. According to this myth, the Taj Mahal was designed to reflect the grandeur of the Mughal dynasty and to serve as a statement to future generations of the empire's wealth, cultural achievements, and architectural prowess. In this version of events, the love story between Shah Jahan and Mumtaz Mahal is secondary to the emperor's desire to immortalize his reign through an enduring monument. While it is true that the Taj Mahal stands as a testament to the artistic and architectural achievements of the Mughal Empire, most historians agree that Shah Jahan's primary motivation was his deep love for Mumtaz Mahal. The monument's grandeur and beauty were undoubtedly intended to reflect the glory of the Mughal Empire, but the personal, emotional connection between the emperor and his wife remains the central narrative behind the Taj Mahal's creation.

Perhaps the most enduring myth of all is the idea that the Taj Mahal is somehow timeless, existing outside the normal constraints of history and mortality. This myth is perpetuated by the monument's almost otherworldly beauty and the fact that it has remained relatively well-preserved over the centuries. Despite being over 350 years old, the Taj Mahal continues to captivate visitors with its pristine white marble, its symmetrical design, and its serene atmosphere. The myth of the Taj Mahal's timelessness is also reinforced by the fact that it is a mausoleum—a place where time seems to stand still, and the boundary between life and death is blurred. In this sense, the Taj Mahal has become a symbol of eternity, not just in terms of the love between Shah Jahan and Mumtaz Mahal but also in its ability to transcend the ravages of time and remain an enduring icon of beauty and devotion.

These myths and legends, while not historically accurate, have become an integral part of the Taj Mahal's cultural and symbolic identity. They add layers of meaning to the monument, allowing people from different backgrounds and time periods to connect with it in unique and personal ways. Whether viewed as a symbol of eternal love, a masterpiece of Mughal architecture, or a monument shrouded in mystery and legend, the Taj Mahal continues to inspire wonder and fascination, its myths serving as a testament to its enduring appeal and significance in the world's collective imagination.

Chapter 10: How the Taj Mahal Was Protected Over Time

The Taj Mahal, one of the world's most iconic and beloved architectural wonders, has withstood the test of time not only as a symbol of eternal love but also as a masterpiece of human craftsmanship. Over the centuries, this monument to love has faced various threats, ranging from environmental degradation and natural disasters to wars and political upheavals. Despite these challenges, considerable efforts have been made to protect, preserve, and maintain the Taj Mahal's magnificence. These efforts reflect the monument's immense cultural, historical, and architectural value. Understanding how the Taj Mahal has been protected over time offers insight into the challenges of safeguarding such an iconic structure while preserving its legacy for future generations.

One of the earliest challenges to the Taj Mahal's protection came soon after its completion in the mid-17th century. The Mughal Empire, at the height of its power under Shah Jahan, who commissioned the monument, was beginning to experience internal political struggles and external threats from rival kingdoms. As the empire weakened, the Taj Mahal, like many other monuments of the time, faced the possibility of neglect. Shah Jahan's reign ended with his imprisonment by his son Aurangzeb, who was more focused on expanding the empire than preserving its architectural marvels. Although Aurangzeb allowed the monument to remain intact, little attention was given to its upkeep during his reign, and the surrounding structures and gardens began to suffer from neglect. However, even during these turbulent times, the Taj Mahal's status as a symbol of the Mughal dynasty's greatness helped protect it from deliberate destruction.

During the 18th century, the Mughal Empire further declined, and the Taj Mahal found itself in the midst of conflict between various warring factions. The region surrounding the monument became a battleground for local rulers, European colonial powers, and invading forces. One of the most significant threats during this period came from the Jats, a warrior group from northern India who raided Agra and reportedly plundered precious gems and decorations from the Taj Mahal. According to some accounts, they removed silver doors and other valuable materials from the monument, causing significant damage to its intricate inlay work and ornamental features. The Jats' looting represented one of the earliest instances of the Taj Mahal being physically harmed by human actions, highlighting the vulnerability of such a monumental structure during times of political instability.

The arrival of the British in India in the 18th and 19th centuries posed both threats and opportunities for the Taj Mahal's preservation. On the one hand, British colonial authorities were known for their disdain for Mughal architecture and often used historical monuments for utilitarian purposes. The Taj Mahal was not immune to this disregard, as British officials reportedly considered using the monument's marble for construction projects. Some sources claim that Lord William Bentinck, the then-Governor-General of India, even entertained the idea of auctioning off the Taj Mahal's marble. Although this plan never came to fruition, the fact that it was considered highlights the precarious position the monument occupied during the early days of British rule. On the other hand, the British also played a role in protecting the Taj Mahal from further degradation. By the mid-19th century, British officials began to recognize the cultural and historical value of the Taj Mahal and took steps to restore and preserve the monument.

One of the earliest restoration efforts came under British supervision during the reign of Lord Curzon, who served as Viceroy of India from 1899 to 1905. Curzon, an ardent admirer of Indian art and architecture, was deeply concerned about the condition of the Taj Mahal, which had suffered from years of neglect, pollution, and natural wear and tear. He spearheaded a major restoration project aimed at restoring the monument's beauty and grandeur. Curzon's efforts included repairing damaged marble, restoring the monument's intricate inlay work, and revitalizing the gardens that had fallen into disrepair. He also introduced policies aimed at protecting the Taj Mahal from further damage, including limiting access to certain parts of the monument to prevent wear and tear caused by visitors. While Curzon's restoration efforts have been criticized for their imperialist overtones and heavy-handedness, they played a crucial role in preserving the Taj Mahal for future generations.

The 20th century saw new challenges for the protection of the Taj Mahal, particularly during the period of World War II and the subsequent political upheavals in India. During World War II, the Taj Mahal faced the very real threat of aerial bombing. The British, who were still in control of India at the time, took measures to camouflage the monument to protect it from potential attacks. They used bamboo scaffolding to cover the structure, making it blend into the surrounding landscape and less visible from the air. This effort to disguise the Taj Mahal was largely successful, as the monument was not targeted during the war. However, this period highlighted the vulnerability of the Taj Mahal to modern warfare and the importance of proactive measures to protect it from external threats.

After India gained independence in 1947, the Taj Mahal became a national symbol of India's cultural heritage. The newly independent Indian government took steps to ensure that the monument was preserved and maintained. The Archaeological Survey of India (ASI), which had been established by the British in the 19th century, was tasked with overseeing the conservation and restoration of the Taj Mahal. Under the ASI's supervision, the monument underwent several rounds of restoration, including cleaning and repairing the marble, maintaining the inlay work, and ensuring the structural integrity of the building. The Indian government also introduced legislation to protect the Taj Mahal and other historical monuments from damage, pollution, and unauthorized construction in the surrounding areas. These efforts were aimed at preserving the monument for future generations while ensuring that it remained a symbol of India's rich cultural heritage.

However, the 20th century also brought new environmental challenges that threatened the Taj Mahal's preservation. Rapid industrialization and urbanization in the region surrounding Agra led to increased levels of air pollution, which began to take a toll on the white marble of the Taj Mahal. The marble started to show signs of yellowing and deterioration due to exposure to pollutants such as sulfur dioxide, which mixed with moisture in the air to form acid rain. This acid rain reacted with the marble, causing it to lose its shine and erode over time. The Indian government recognized the severity of the problem and took steps to mitigate the effects of pollution on the Taj Mahal. In 1996, the Indian Supreme Court ordered the closure or relocation of numerous factories and industrial plants in the vicinity of the monument. Additionally, the government created a "Taj Trapezium Zone," a protected area around the Taj Mahal where certain activities, such as industrial emissions, vehicle exhaust, and construction, were restricted to reduce pollution levels.

Despite these measures, pollution remains an ongoing concern for the Taj Mahal's long-term preservation. In recent years, the government has introduced new initiatives aimed at reducing the impact of pollution on the monument. These efforts include the use of eco-friendly electric vehicles to transport visitors to and from the site, regular cleaning of the marble using a special clay pack treatment known as "Multani mitti," and the installation of air quality monitoring stations to track pollution levels in the area. These modern preservation techniques reflect the continued commitment to protecting the Taj Mahal from the environmental threats posed by industrialization and urbanization.

Another significant challenge for the protection of the Taj Mahal has been the threat of flooding and water damage. The monument is located near the Yamuna River, which has historically been prone to flooding. In recent years, concerns have been raised about the declining water levels in the river, which could impact the stability of the Taj Mahal's foundation. The river's water once provided natural moisture that helped maintain the stability of the wooden foundation beneath the monument. However, with the decreasing water levels, the foundation could potentially weaken, posing a threat to the structural integrity of the Taj Mahal. To address this issue, the Indian government has initiated studies to assess the impact of the river's water levels on the monument and explore ways to mitigate any potential damage. These efforts highlight the importance of not only protecting the visible parts of the Taj Mahal but also ensuring the stability of its underlying foundation.

The rise of tourism in recent decades has also posed challenges for the preservation of the Taj Mahal. Millions of visitors from around the world come to see the monument each year, and the sheer volume of foot traffic has the potential to cause wear and tear to the structure. To protect the Taj Mahal from the impact of tourism, the Indian government has implemented various measures, including limiting the number of visitors allowed inside the main mausoleum at any given time, restricting access to certain areas, and requiring visitors to wear shoe covers when entering the monument to prevent damage to the marble floors. Additionally, the government has taken steps to manage the flow of tourists around the site by creating designated walkways and viewing areas to minimize the impact on the monument itself. These efforts are aimed at striking a balance between allowing visitors to experience the beauty of the Taj Mahal while ensuring that it remains protected for future generations.

In recent years, the Taj Mahal has also faced the threat of climate change, which has the potential to exacerbate existing environmental challenges and create new ones. Rising temperatures, changes in rainfall patterns, and the increased frequency of extreme weather events could all impact the long-term preservation of the monument. In response to these challenges, the Indian government, along with international organizations such as UNESCO, has been working on developing strategies to protect the Taj Mahal from the effects of climate change. These strategies include continued efforts to reduce pollution in the surrounding area, monitoring the structural stability of the monument, and ensuring that the Taj Mahal is prepared to withstand the changing environmental conditions.

Throughout its history, the Taj Mahal has faced numerous challenges, but the concerted efforts of governments, conservationists, and the public have ensured that it remains one of the most well-preserved historical monuments in the world. The story of how the Taj Mahal has been protected over time is a testament to the monument's cultural and historical significance, as well as the enduring commitment to preserving this iconic symbol of love and beauty for future generations. Despite the challenges that lie ahead, the continued efforts to protect and preserve the Taj Mahal will undoubtedly ensure that it remains a source of inspiration and wonder for centuries to come.

Chapter 11: The Calligraphy on the Taj Mahal

The calligraphy on the Taj Mahal is one of the most intricate and mesmerizing features of the monument, adding a profound sense of artistry and spirituality to the structure. The calligraphy is primarily composed of verses from the Quran, Islam's holy book, and it serves as a decorative element as well as a spiritual guide, encouraging contemplation of the divine. The black inscriptions are laid out in an elegant script known as Thuluth, a highly artistic form of Arabic script, which was widely used during the Mughal period for religious and ceremonial purposes due to its fluid, majestic, and dynamic lines.

One of the key aspects of the calligraphy is how it has been masterfully designed to maintain a sense of proportion and readability, even when viewed from different distances. This is achieved through a technique known as "anamorphic scaling." When you look at the calligraphy from the ground, it appears uniformly sized, but in reality, the letters near the top of the arches and domes are significantly larger than those at the bottom. This clever manipulation of scale allows the inscriptions to appear consistent and harmonious to the viewer from various angles, ensuring that the spiritual messages of the Quran can be read clearly from below. This technique highlights the incredible craftsmanship and attention to detail employed by the artisans who worked on the Taj Mahal.

The verses inscribed on the Taj Mahal are carefully chosen, often emphasizing themes of paradise, divine mercy, and eternal peace. These themes resonate deeply with the purpose of the monument itself, which is a mausoleum built by Emperor Shah Jahan in memory of his beloved wife, Mumtaz Mahal. By adorning the structure with Quranic verses that speak of the afterlife and divine grace, the calligraphy becomes more than mere decoration—it imbues the entire monument with a sense of sanctity and eternal love. The passages convey a message of solace, reminding those who visit that death is not the end, but a gateway to a higher, more peaceful existence.

The most prominent location for the calligraphy is the main entrance gate, also known as the Great Gate or "Darwaza-i-Rauza." As you approach the Taj Mahal, the first thing you encounter is this grand gateway, which is lavishly decorated with inscriptions from the Quran. One of the most notable inscriptions here is a verse that invites the faithful to enter paradise, a fitting message as visitors cross the threshold into the serene and sacred grounds of the Taj Mahal. This inscription sets the tone for the entire visit, encouraging a sense of reverence and reflection.

In addition to the Great Gate, calligraphy adorns the cenotaphs inside the central chamber, where the false tombs of Mumtaz Mahal and Shah Jahan are placed. The actual graves are located in a crypt beneath the chamber, but the cenotaphs are the focal point for visitors. The calligraphy around the cenotaphs is more intimate, with verses that speak of God's mercy and the promise of paradise. This reinforces the idea that the Taj Mahal is not just a monument of earthly love, but also a spiritual symbol, connecting the temporal world with the eternal.

The craftsmanship of the calligraphy was entrusted to a master calligrapher named Amanat Khan, who was renowned for his skill and artistry. Amanat Khan's role in the construction of the Taj Mahal was so crucial that his name is the only one that appears on the monument. His signature can be found on one of the panels at the base of the structure, a rare and significant honor in the Islamic art world, where personal recognition is often secondary to the collective achievement of the artisans. Amanat Khan's work on the Taj Mahal stands as a testament to the precision, dedication, and spiritual devotion that went into every aspect of the monument's design.

The black marble used for the calligraphy is inlaid into the white marble of the Taj Mahal, creating a striking contrast that enhances the readability and visual impact of the inscriptions. This technique, known as "parchinkari" or inlay work, was a hallmark of Mughal architecture, reflecting the empire's rich tradition of combining different artistic techniques and materials to create something truly unique and magnificent. The use of black marble against the gleaming white surface gives the calligraphy a sense of permanence and gravitas, making the words of the Quran seem as though they are an integral part of the structure itself.

Beyond its spiritual and aesthetic significance, the calligraphy on the Taj Mahal also reflects the cultural and intellectual milieu of the Mughal Empire, a period known for its deep appreciation of literature, art, and religious thought. The Mughals were great patrons of Islamic art, and the calligraphy on the Taj Mahal is a prime example of how art and architecture were used to express both personal devotion and imperial grandeur. The inscriptions are not just religious symbols; they are a reflection of the Mughal Empire's dedication to beauty, knowledge, and the divine. In this way, the calligraphy on the Taj Mahal serves as a bridge between the earthly and the divine, between the personal and the universal.

Interestingly, the calligraphy on the Taj Mahal has not only survived the passage of time but has also inspired countless other works of Islamic architecture and art. The precision and elegance of the inscriptions have been studied and admired by scholars and artists alike, and they continue to be a source of inspiration for those who seek to understand the deep connections between art, religion, and architecture in the Islamic world. The way the calligraphy enhances the spiritual atmosphere of the Taj Mahal has become a model for how sacred spaces can be adorned with text in a way that amplifies both their aesthetic and spiritual resonance.

Over time, the calligraphy on the Taj Mahal has come to symbolize not just the monument itself but also the broader cultural heritage of the Mughal period. It stands as a reminder of the incredible skill of the artisans who worked on the monument and the profound spiritual vision that guided its creation. For visitors, the inscriptions offer a moment of reflection, a chance to connect with the deeper meanings behind the beauty of the Taj Mahal. In this sense, the calligraphy is not just a decorative element—it is a vital part of the monument's enduring legacy.

The calligraphy continues to evoke a sense of wonder and admiration for those who visit the Taj Mahal. Whether viewed up close or from afar, the inscriptions draw the eye and invite contemplation. They serve as a reminder of the power of words, art, and faith to transcend time and space, connecting generations of people across centuries. As long as the Taj Mahal stands, its calligraphy will continue to speak to those who seek to understand the profound relationship between love, faith, and beauty that the monument so perfectly embodies.

Chapter 12: The Symbolism of the Taj Mahal's Design

The symbolism of the Taj Mahal's design goes far beyond its stunning physical beauty. Every element of this majestic monument is laden with deeper meaning, reflecting the philosophical, religious, and cultural ideas of the Mughal Empire, as well as the personal emotions that inspired its creation. Built by Emperor Shah Jahan in memory of his beloved wife Mumtaz Mahal, the Taj Mahal is often described as an eternal symbol of love, but its design also expresses themes of paradise, the afterlife, divine justice, and the perfection of God's creation. Understanding the rich symbolism embedded in the architecture allows us to appreciate the Taj Mahal not just as an iconic monument, but as a profound work of art that carries multiple layers of meaning.

The overall structure of the Taj Mahal can be interpreted as a physical representation of paradise on Earth. In Islamic tradition, paradise is often described as a lush, symmetrical garden filled with water channels, trees, and flowers, where souls are at peace in the presence of the divine. The layout of the Taj Mahal mirrors these descriptions. It sits within a large, formal garden known as a "charbagh," a type of garden that is divided into four quadrants by walkways and water channels. This symmetrical design represents the four rivers of paradise mentioned in the Quran, which flow with water, milk, wine, and honey. The Taj Mahal's charbagh, with its carefully manicured lawns, flowering plants, and reflecting pools, creates a serene, otherworldly atmosphere that is meant to evoke the eternal peace and harmony of paradise.

At the center of this garden stands the Taj Mahal itself, gleaming white and perfectly symmetrical, symbolizing the throne of God in the Islamic conception of the afterlife. The white marble, chosen for its purity and radiance, reflects the divine light and suggests the spiritual purity of the souls it houses. The monument's symmetry, where every side mirrors the other, reinforces the idea of divine perfection. The balance and harmony in the design are not just a reflection of aesthetic principles, but a symbol of the balance and order of the universe as created by God. For the Mughals, who were deeply influenced by Islamic teachings, symmetry in architecture was a way of expressing their belief in a universe that is orderly, harmonious, and ruled by divine law.

The central dome of the Taj Mahal, which rises majestically above the rest of the structure, is one of its most iconic features. In Islamic architecture, domes often symbolize the vault of heaven. The shape of the dome mirrors the sky, creating a connection between the earthly and the celestial realms. This is especially significant in the context of the Taj Mahal, which is not only a mausoleum but also a spiritual symbol of the journey from life to death and, ultimately, to eternal life in the presence of God. The dome, with its smooth, unbroken curve, suggests the infinite nature of the divine, while its sheer size and prominence signify the monument's importance as a place of rest for the emperor's beloved wife, as well as a representation of the eternal love they shared.

The four minarets that surround the central dome also carry symbolic meaning. In traditional Islamic architecture, minarets are typically used for the call to prayer, and their presence here reinforces the spiritual significance of the Taj Mahal. However, their arrangement at the four corners of the platform that holds the mausoleum has a deeper symbolic resonance. The number four holds special meaning in Islamic culture, often representing completeness and stability. By placing the minarets symmetrically around the tomb, the architects created a sense of cosmic order, with the tomb at the center of the universe. The minarets also serve a practical purpose in reinforcing the monument's symmetry, which is a key symbolic feature throughout the design.

Another symbolic element of the Taj Mahal is the use of light and shadow in its design. The changing light throughout the day dramatically alters the appearance of the monument, symbolizing the passage of time and the transient nature of life. In the early morning, the Taj Mahal glows with a soft pink hue, while at sunset, it takes on a golden tone. At night, under the light of the full moon, it seems to glow from within. This constant transformation of the monument's appearance reflects the idea that life is fleeting and ever-changing, but that love, like the Taj Mahal itself, endures beyond the physical world. The interplay of light and shadow also echoes the spiritual journey from the darkness of the earthly realm to the divine light of the afterlife.

The materials used in the construction of the Taj Mahal further enhance its symbolism. White marble, chosen for the main structure, symbolizes purity, spirituality, and the eternal. In contrast, the red sandstone used for the surrounding buildings, such as the mosque and guesthouse, represents the earthy, temporal world. Together, these contrasting materials symbolize the duality of life and death, the material and the spiritual, the earthly and the divine. The use of precious stones, such as jasper, jade, and lapis lazuli, in the inlay work throughout the monument adds another layer of meaning. These stones were chosen not only for their beauty but for their symbolic associations with heaven, immortality, and protection from evil.

The inlay work, known as "parchinkari," that adorns the Taj Mahal is one of its most exquisite features and carries deep symbolic meaning. Floral motifs are a dominant theme in the inlay designs, with delicate flowers and vines meticulously carved into the marble and inlaid with precious stones. These floral patterns symbolize the gardens of paradise, reinforcing the idea that the Taj Mahal is a representation of heaven on Earth. In Islamic art, flowers also represent the fragility and transience of life, reminding viewers of the impermanence of the physical world and the eternity of the spiritual realm. The intricate detail of the inlay work reflects the care and devotion that went into the creation of the monument, much like the love that inspired its construction.

Even the inscriptions on the Taj Mahal carry symbolic weight. The Quranic verses inscribed in elegant calligraphy on the monument's walls emphasize themes of paradise, divine mercy, and the eternal. These inscriptions remind visitors that the Taj Mahal is not just a tomb, but a place where the earthly and the divine intersect. The words of the Quran, carefully selected for their spiritual significance, invite contemplation of the afterlife and the promise of eternal peace for those who enter paradise. The calligraphy is not only a decorative element but a profound reminder of the spiritual journey that the monument represents.

The reflection of the Taj Mahal in the water of the long pool that runs through the center of the garden adds another layer of symbolism to the design. The reflection creates a mirror image of the monument, suggesting the idea of duality: life and death, love and loss, the earthly and the divine. This duality is a central theme in the symbolism of the Taj Mahal's design. The reflection also creates a sense of illusion, as though the Taj Mahal is floating on water or suspended between heaven and earth, further enhancing its otherworldly atmosphere.

Finally, the very purpose of the Taj Mahal as a mausoleum adds to its symbolic significance. Built as a testament to Shah Jahan's love for Mumtaz Mahal, the monument is often seen as the ultimate expression of love that transcends death. While the physical bodies of the emperor and his wife are entombed within the Taj Mahal, the monument itself stands as a symbol of the enduring nature of their love. In this sense, the Taj Mahal is not just a symbol of earthly love, but of eternal love, which, like the monument, endures beyond time and death. The fact that the Taj Mahal has stood the test of time, remaining one of the most admired and beloved structures in the world, reinforces this idea of eternal love and beauty.

In conclusion, the symbolism of the Taj Mahal's design is incredibly rich and multi-layered. From its representation of paradise to its evocation of divine perfection, from its reflection of the spiritual journey to its expression of eternal love, every element of the monument is imbued with meaning. The architects and artisans who created the Taj Mahal did more than just build a beautiful structure—they crafted a work of art that speaks to the deepest human emotions and beliefs about life, death, and the eternal.

Chapter 13: The Role of the Taj Mahal in Indian History

The role of the Taj Mahal in Indian history is not just limited to its status as one of the world's most beautiful and iconic structures, but also as a symbol of the rich cultural, political, and architectural heritage of India. Built during the height of the Mughal Empire in the mid-17th century, the Taj Mahal stands as a testament to the artistic and intellectual achievements of this powerful dynasty. Its creation is intertwined with the personal story of Emperor Shah Jahan and his deep love for his wife, Mumtaz Mahal, but it also reflects the broader historical and cultural currents of its time, including the Mughal Empire's vision of kingship, their synthesis of diverse cultural and religious influences, and their profound impact on Indian society.

The Taj Mahal was commissioned by Shah Jahan in 1631, following the death of his beloved wife Mumtaz Mahal, who passed away while giving birth to their 14th child. Devastated by her loss, Shah Jahan vowed to create a monument that would honor her memory and reflect the grandeur of their love. The construction of the Taj Mahal began in 1632 and continued for more than two decades, involving thousands of artisans, craftsmen, and laborers from across the empire and beyond. The monument's completion in 1653 was a triumph of Mughal engineering, design, and artistry, representing not only a personal memorial but also a political statement of Shah Jahan's power, wealth, and vision as a ruler.

In terms of Indian history, the Taj Mahal is deeply connected to the legacy of the Mughal Empire, one of the most powerful and influential empires in Indian history. The Mughals, who were of Turko-Mongol descent, ruled large parts of the Indian subcontinent from the early 16th century until the early 18th century, and their influence on Indian culture, politics, and society was profound. The empire was known for its sophisticated administrative system, its promotion of trade and culture, and its ability to bring together diverse religious and ethnic communities under a relatively stable and prosperous regime. The Taj Mahal, as a product of the Mughal period, exemplifies the empire's architectural genius, but it also reflects its political and cultural ambitions.

One of the key ways in which the Taj Mahal represents the Mughal Empire's role in Indian history is through its fusion of various architectural and artistic traditions. The Mughals were known for their ability to synthesize Persian, Islamic, Turkish, and Indian influences in their art and architecture, and the Taj Mahal is a prime example of this cultural blending. The structure's design draws heavily on Persian architectural elements, such as the use of large, symmetrical gardens and the central dome, which were characteristic features of Persian imperial buildings. At the same time, the Taj Mahal incorporates elements of traditional Indian architecture, including the use of inlay work (called "parchinkari") and certain decorative motifs. This blending of styles reflects the Mughal Empire's cosmopolitan nature and its ability to bring together diverse cultural influences into a unified and harmonious whole, which was a key aspect of Mughal rule in India.

The religious symbolism of the Taj Mahal also reflects the Mughal approach to governance and society. While the Mughals were Muslims, they ruled over a predominantly Hindu population and made efforts to create a more inclusive and pluralistic society. The Taj Mahal, while primarily an Islamic structure, is imbued with symbolism that speaks to both Islamic and broader religious traditions. For example, the layout of the gardens and the use of water channels evoke the Islamic concept of paradise, but the emphasis on balance, harmony, and the blending of natural and built environments also resonates with Hindu and Buddhist ideas about the relationship between humans and the divine. In this sense, the Taj Mahal can be seen as a reflection of the Mughal

Empire's efforts to create a more harmonious and integrated society, where different religious and cultural traditions could coexist.

The Taj Mahal also played a significant role in shaping perceptions of Indian kingship and imperial power during the Mughal period. Shah Jahan, like many Mughal rulers, saw himself as both a political leader and a divinely appointed representative of God on Earth. The grandeur and scale of the Taj Mahal were intended to reflect Shah Jahan's status as a ruler chosen by divine will and to project his power and authority to his subjects and rivals alike. The monument's massive size, its use of expensive materials such as white marble and precious stones, and its meticulous craftsmanship all conveyed a message of imperial splendor and invincibility. In this way, the Taj Mahal served not only as a personal tribute to Shah Jahan's wife but also as a political statement about his own power and legitimacy as emperor.

In the broader context of Indian history, the Taj Mahal has come to symbolize the apex of Mughal art and architecture, as well as the empire's broader contributions to Indian culture. The Mughal period is often regarded as a golden age of Indian architecture, and the Taj Mahal, as one of the most famous examples of Mughal architecture, epitomizes this era of cultural and artistic flourishing. The techniques and styles developed by Mughal architects and artisans during the construction of the Taj Mahal influenced subsequent generations of Indian builders and artists, and many of these techniques continue to be used in Indian architecture today. The legacy of the Mughal Empire's architectural achievements is particularly visible in the design of later Indian palaces, mosques, and tombs, which often incorporate elements of Mughal style.

The Taj Mahal's role in Indian history also extends beyond the Mughal period. After the decline of the Mughal Empire in the early 18th century, the Taj Mahal, like many other Mughal monuments, fell into a state of disrepair. During the 19th century, under British colonial rule, efforts were made to restore and preserve the Taj Mahal, as British officials came to see it as a symbol of India's rich cultural heritage. The British restoration of the Taj Mahal was part of a broader effort to present themselves as the rightful heirs to India's imperial legacy, and the monument became a key site for British colonial tourism. The British fascination with the Taj Mahal helped to raise its profile internationally, and it became an important symbol of India's architectural and cultural achievements in the eyes of the world.

In the modern era, the Taj Mahal has continued to play a significant role in Indian national identity and heritage. Following India's independence in 1947, the Taj Mahal was embraced as a symbol of the nation's rich cultural past, and it became one of the most important tourist attractions in the country. The monument's status as a UNESCO World Heritage Site, which was granted in 1983, further cemented its reputation as a global icon of Indian culture. Today, the Taj Mahal is not only a major source of national pride but also an economic asset, drawing millions of visitors from around the world each year. Its image is used in everything from advertising to government promotions, and it remains one of the most recognizable symbols of India worldwide.

In Indian political history, the Taj Mahal has also taken on new meanings in the post-independence period. For some, the monument represents the complex legacy of India's Muslim rulers and the country's long history of religious diversity. As a product of the Mughal period, the Taj Mahal stands as a reminder of the contributions of Muslim rulers and architects to Indian culture, challenging narratives that seek to portray India's history as solely Hindu. However, the Taj Mahal has also been a site of political controversy in recent years, with some nationalist groups attempting to downplay or even erase its significance as a symbol of India's Muslim past. Despite these controversies, the Taj Mahal continues to be widely regarded as one of India's most important cultural landmarks, and it remains a powerful symbol of the country's rich and diverse heritage.

Moreover, the Taj Mahal has played a role in shaping international perceptions of India. Since its completion, the monument has attracted the attention of travelers, artists, and writers from around the world, many of whom have marveled at its beauty and grandeur. European travelers in the 17th and 18th centuries wrote extensively about the Taj Mahal, helping to establish its reputation as one of the world's great architectural wonders. In the 19th and 20th centuries, as photography and mass media began to spread, the image of the Taj Mahal became even more widely known, solidifying its place as a global icon of beauty, love, and cultural achievement. Today, the Taj Mahal is often seen as a symbol not just of India's past but of its global cultural influence and soft power.

In conclusion, the role of the Taj Mahal in Indian history is multifaceted and profound. It is a symbol of the Mughal Empire's political power, artistic genius, and cultural synthesis, as well as a reflection of the empire's efforts to create a more harmonious and integrated society. It has shaped perceptions of kingship, power, and imperial grandeur in India, and it continues to influence Indian architecture and culture to this day. Throughout history, the Taj Mahal has served as a symbol of India's rich cultural heritage, a source of national pride, and a global icon of beauty and love. Its enduring legacy speaks to its significance not only as a historical monument but as a living part of India's cultural identity and history.

Chapter 14: The Workers Who Built the Taj Mahal

The Taj Mahal, often considered one of the greatest architectural masterpieces in the world, stands as a testament to the skill, dedication, and artistry of the thousands of workers who helped bring Shah Jahan's grand vision to life. The construction of the Taj Mahal was a colossal effort, requiring the labor of artisans, craftsmen, architects, engineers, and unskilled workers from across the vast Mughal Empire and beyond. The scale of the project, which took more than two decades to complete, necessitated an enormous and highly specialized workforce, whose expertise spanned numerous disciplines, from stone carving and inlay work to the precise engineering of the monument's massive dome and foundations. Understanding the workers who built the Taj Mahal not only illuminates the technical brilliance of this iconic monument but also sheds light on the often overlooked labor force that contributed to one of the greatest achievements of Indian history.

The construction of the Taj Mahal began in 1632, a year after the death of Shah Jahan's beloved wife, Mumtaz Mahal, and continued for over 20 years. During this time, a staggering number of workers were involved in the project. Historical accounts suggest that the workforce at the Taj Mahal's construction site numbered around 20,000 people at its peak. These workers came from various parts of the Mughal Empire, which at the time stretched across much of the Indian subcontinent, and from other regions with a long tradition of skilled craftsmanship, including Persia (modern-day Iran), Central Asia, and even Europe. Each of these workers brought unique skills and expertise to the project, contributing to the creation of a monument that reflects a fusion of architectural and artistic traditions.

The labor force that built the Taj Mahal can be divided into several key groups, each playing a crucial role in different stages of the project.

At the heart of the endeavor were the architects and engineers responsible for designing and overseeing the construction of the monument. The chief architect is widely believed to have been Ustad Ahmad Lahauri, a Persian-born architect who had previously worked on several other Mughal projects. However, the design of the Taj Mahal was likely a collaborative effort, with multiple architects contributing ideas based on Persian, Islamic, Indian, and even European influences. These architects had the daunting task of creating a structure that would not only be visually stunning but also structurally sound enough to last for centuries. They were responsible for calculating the proportions, ensuring the monument's symmetry, and designing its complex systems of support, including the massive central dome, the four minarets, and the intricate inlay work that would adorn its walls.

Alongside the architects, a team of highly skilled engineers was responsible for the technical aspects of the project, including the design of the foundations, the management of water systems for the gardens, and the creation of scaffolding and tools to aid in the construction of the monument. One of the most impressive engineering feats was the construction of the Taj Mahal's massive dome, which rises over 240 feet above the ground. The engineers had to develop innovative techniques to lift and position the heavy stone blocks used to create the dome, and they also devised a system of support structures to ensure that the weight of the dome was evenly distributed. The engineers were also responsible for constructing the four minarets that flank the monument, which were designed with a slight outward tilt to prevent them from collapsing onto the main structure in the event of an earthquake.

One of the most critical groups of workers involved in the construction of the Taj Mahal was the masons and stonecutters. These skilled laborers were responsible for cutting, shaping, and assembling the vast quantities of stone used in the monument's construction. The primary material used for the Taj Mahal was white marble, which was quarried from the Makrana mines in Rajasthan, located over 200 miles away. Transporting this heavy marble to the construction site required an extensive network of carts, elephants, and oxen, and the stonecutters then had to carefully shape each block to ensure a precise fit. The marble used in the Taj Mahal was known for its purity and fine grain, which allowed the stonecutters to achieve the smooth, polished surfaces that give the monument its characteristic glow in the sunlight.

In addition to white marble, other types of stone were used to enhance the beauty of the Taj Mahal. Red sandstone, for example, was used for the construction of the mosque and guesthouse that flank the main mausoleum. Skilled stonecutters from across India worked on these sections of the project, carving intricate patterns and designs into the sandstone to create a contrast with the gleaming white marble of the central structure. The use of contrasting materials and colors was a hallmark of Mughal architecture, and the stonecutters' ability to work with different types of stone added to the monument's visual appeal.

The most famous and admired aspect of the Taj Mahal's design is the intricate inlay work, or "parchinkari," that decorates its walls and surfaces. This inlay work involved the placement of thousands of semi-precious stones, including jasper, lapis lazuli, jade, turquoise, and amethyst, into the marble to create intricate floral and geometric patterns. The artisans responsible for this painstaking work were some of the most skilled craftsmen in the world at the time. They came from various regions known for their expertise in inlay techniques, including Persia and Central Asia. These artisans would first carve out the designs in the marble, creating shallow cavities into which the stones would be fitted. Each piece of stone had to be carefully cut and polished to match the shape of the cavity, and then it was secured in place with a special adhesive. The precision required for this work was extraordinary, and even the smallest mistake could ruin the entire design.

The inlay work on the Taj Mahal is not only a testament to the technical skill of the artisans but also to their artistic creativity. The floral motifs, which were inspired by both Persian and Indian traditions, symbolize the gardens of paradise and add a sense of liveliness and movement to the otherwise solid and imposing structure. The geometric patterns, which are characteristic of Islamic art, reflect the Mughal Empire's emphasis on order, harmony, and balance. Together, these designs create a sense of unity and coherence, which is one of the defining features of the Taj Mahal's overall aesthetic.

Another group of workers who played a crucial role in the construction of the Taj Mahal was the calligraphers. The monument is adorned with verses from the Quran, written in elegant Arabic script, which are inscribed on the walls, arches, and entrance gates. The calligraphy is not only a religious feature but also a decorative element that enhances the beauty of the monument. The chief calligrapher responsible for this work was Amanat Khan, a Persian master of the art of Islamic calligraphy. The calligraphers used black marble or onyx to create the script, which contrasts sharply with the white marble background. The inscriptions were meticulously crafted, with the size of the letters increasing as they ascend higher up the walls, creating an optical illusion that makes them appear uniform from the ground.

Beyond the skilled artisans and craftsmen, a large number of unskilled laborers were also involved in the construction of the Taj Mahal. These workers, who came from various regions of the Mughal Empire, were responsible for transporting materials, mixing mortar, and carrying out the heavy lifting and manual labor required for such a massive project. Many of these laborers were local villagers or migrants who came to Agra, where the Taj Mahal is located, in search of work. While their contributions may not have been as specialized as those of the architects or artisans, their labor was essential to the completion of the monument. Without the hard work and perseverance of these thousands of laborers, the Taj Mahal would not have been possible.

The logistics of organizing and managing such a large and diverse workforce were also a significant challenge. The construction of the

Taj Mahal required careful planning and coordination, with different groups of workers working on various parts of the project simultaneously. Supervisors, many of whom were skilled craftsmen or engineers themselves, oversaw the work and ensured that each stage of construction was completed to the highest standards. In addition to the technical challenges, the project also required a massive supply of materials, which had to be sourced from across the Mughal Empire and beyond. These materials included not only marble and precious stones but also bricks, lime, and timber for scaffolding.

The workers who built the Taj Mahal lived in temporary camps near the construction site, and their living conditions varied depending on their rank and level of skill. Skilled artisans and architects were often provided with better accommodations and food, while unskilled laborers lived in more basic conditions. Despite the challenges and hardships they faced, the workers were motivated by the prestige of working on such an important imperial project and by the knowledge that their work would be admired for generations to come.

The completion of the Taj Mahal in 1653 marked the culmination of years of effort by these thousands of workers. The monument, with its perfect symmetry, gleaming white marble, and intricate decorative details, was an extraordinary achievement, made possible by the collaboration of individuals from different cultures, regions, and backgrounds. The workers who built the Taj Mahal left behind a legacy of craftsmanship and artistry that continues to inspire awe and admiration to this day.

In conclusion, the construction of the Taj Mahal was a monumental undertaking that required the labor and expertise of thousands of workers from across the Mughal Empire and beyond. From architects and engineers to stonecutters, inlay artisans, calligraphers, and unskilled laborers, each group played a crucial role in bringing Shah Jahan's vision to life. The workers who built the Taj Mahal were not only masters of their craft but also innovators who developed new techniques and approaches to meet the challenges of constructing such a large and complex structure. Their contributions helped create one of the world's most beautiful and enduring monuments, a symbol of love, beauty, and the artistic genius of the Mughal Empire.

Chapter 15: The Taj Mahal's Influence on Art and Architecture

The Taj Mahal's influence on art and architecture is profound and enduring, leaving an indelible mark not only on Indian design but also on the global architectural landscape. Since its completion in 1653, the Taj Mahal has been regarded as one of the finest examples of Mughal architecture, a style that represents a synthesis of Islamic, Persian, Indian, and even elements of Turkish and Central Asian architectural traditions. The monument's unique blend of these diverse influences has made it a source of inspiration for architects, artists, and designers across centuries, transcending geographical and cultural boundaries. The Taj Mahal's influence can be traced in the evolution of architectural forms in India and beyond, in both its contemporaneous structures and later constructions, and in how it shaped artistic approaches to themes of symmetry, harmony, beauty, and cultural fusion.

The Taj Mahal's impact on Mughal architecture was immediate and profound, as it represented the culmination of a long evolution in the architectural style of the Mughal Empire. The Mughals were known for their ambitious building projects, and each emperor sought to outdo his predecessor by commissioning ever more elaborate palaces, forts, mosques, and mausoleums. Under Shah Jahan, who commissioned the Taj Mahal, Mughal architecture reached its zenith. His reign saw the refinement of a distinct architectural vocabulary that combined Persian elegance with Indian craftsmanship and Islamic principles of design. The Taj Mahal, as the most famous building from this period, served as a benchmark for subsequent Mughal projects and for Indian architecture more broadly.

One of the key architectural innovations of the Taj Mahal is its use of symmetry and balance, which became a defining feature of Mughal architecture and influenced numerous structures that followed. The layout of the Taj Mahal complex is meticulously planned, with the main mausoleum positioned at the center of a large formal garden, flanked by a mosque on one side and a guesthouse on the other. The garden is divided into quadrants by four water channels, which are meant to symbolize the rivers of paradise in Islamic tradition. This strict adherence to symmetry, combined with the harmonious proportions of the building's elements—such as the large central dome, the slender minarets, and the detailed inlay work—creates a sense of perfection and serenity that has captivated viewers for centuries.

The Taj Mahal's influence on later Mughal architecture can be seen in other imperial buildings constructed after its completion. For example, the Red Fort in Delhi, also built during Shah Jahan's reign, incorporates similar elements of symmetry, balance, and the use of white marble. The Moti Masjid (Pearl Mosque) in Agra and the Jama Masjid in Delhi, both constructed in the latter half of Shah Jahan's reign, show clear influences from the design principles established at the Taj Mahal. Even Aurangzeb, Shah Jahan's more austere successor, followed many of these principles in his construction of the Bibi Ka Maqbara in Aurangabad, a mausoleum built for his wife that bears a striking resemblance to the Taj Mahal, though it is more modest in scale and ornamentation.

Beyond the Mughal Empire, the Taj Mahal also left a lasting imprint on Indian architecture in subsequent centuries. During the British colonial period in India, the British sought to incorporate elements of Indian architecture into their own building projects, a style known as Indo-Saracenic architecture. The Taj Mahal, along with other Mughal buildings, served as an important source of inspiration for British architects who designed government buildings, palaces, and even railway stations across India. One of the most famous examples of this influence is the Victoria Memorial in Kolkata, which was built between 1906 and 1921 as a tribute to Queen Victoria. The building's white marble façade, central dome, and overall grandeur clearly draw on the aesthetic of the Taj Mahal, though the style is adapted to reflect British tastes and the colonial context.

In addition to its influence on architecture, the Taj Mahal has also had a significant impact on the visual arts. The monument's intricate inlay work, which features detailed floral and geometric patterns made from semi-precious stones, has inspired generations of artisans and craftsmen in India and beyond. This technique, known as "parchinkari," became highly prized and was emulated in other Mughal buildings and in objects such as jewelry, furniture, and textiles. The craftsmanship of the Taj Mahal set a new standard for decorative arts in India, and its influence can still be seen today in the work of modern Indian artisans who continue to practice traditional inlay techniques.

The symbolism and artistry of the Taj Mahal also had a broader cultural impact, shaping artistic representations of love, beauty, and paradise. As a monument built to commemorate Shah Jahan's deep love for his wife Mumtaz Mahal, the Taj Mahal has long been associated with the idea of eternal love and devotion. This theme has been explored in various artistic mediums, including poetry, painting, and literature. The beauty and romanticism of the Taj Mahal have inspired countless artists to depict the monument in their work, often focusing on its ethereal qualities, such as the way the white marble changes color with the shifting light of day or the reflection of the monument in the still waters of the surrounding gardens. These artistic depictions of the Taj Mahal helped to cement its place in the global imagination as a symbol of love and beauty.

The Taj Mahal's influence also extends beyond the borders of India, as it has inspired architects and artists around the world. In the Middle East, particularly in countries with a strong Islamic architectural tradition, the design of the Taj Mahal has served as a model for mosques, palaces, and other monumental buildings. The concept of a large central dome flanked by minarets, which was perfected at the Taj

Mahal, became a popular feature in mosque architecture throughout the Islamic world. The Sultan Ahmed Mosque (Blue Mosque) in Istanbul, though built earlier than the Taj Mahal, shares many design elements with the Mughal structure, such as the use of a large central dome and a symmetrical layout with four minarets.

In Europe, the Taj Mahal became a source of fascination for architects and designers, particularly during the 19th century, when interest in Orientalism and exotic styles was at its peak. The Romantic movement in Europe, with its emphasis on emotion, beauty, and the sublime, found much to admire in the Taj Mahal's design and the love story behind it. European travelers who visited India in the 18th and 19th centuries wrote extensively about the Taj Mahal in their travelogues, often describing it as one of the most beautiful buildings they had ever seen. These accounts helped to popularize the Taj Mahal in Europe and inspired architects to incorporate elements of Mughal architecture into their designs.

The influence of the Taj Mahal can be seen in several European buildings constructed in the 19th century, particularly in the realm of garden and palace design. For example, the Royal Pavilion in Brighton, England, designed by John Nash in the early 19th century, is an eclectic building that combines elements of Mughal, Islamic, and Chinese architecture. Though its design is more fantastical than the restrained elegance of the Taj Mahal, the Pavilion's onion domes and minarets were directly inspired by Mughal architecture, demonstrating the far-reaching impact of the Taj Mahal's design on European aesthetics.

The fascination with the Taj Mahal continued into the 20th century, influencing modern and contemporary architecture in various parts of the world. In the United States, for example, the influence of the Taj Mahal can be seen in the design of the BAPS Shri Swaminarayan Mandir in Chicago, a large Hindu temple complex built in 2004. Though it is a religious building rather than a mausoleum, the temple incorporates many elements reminiscent of the Taj Mahal, such as its white marble façade, intricate inlay work, and symmetrical layout. The use of traditional craftsmanship and attention to detail in the temple's design reflects the enduring legacy of the Taj Mahal's architectural principles.

The Taj Mahal's influence on modern architecture is also evident in the work of contemporary architects who have drawn inspiration from its harmonious proportions, its use of light and space, and its symbolic meaning. Renowned architects such as Zaha Hadid and Sir Norman Foster have cited the Taj Mahal as an influence on their work, particularly in their use of organic forms, fluidity of design, and the integration of natural and built environments. The Taj Mahal's emphasis on balance, harmony, and beauty continues to resonate with architects and designers who seek to create buildings that are not only functional but also aesthetically pleasing and spiritually meaningful.

In the realm of popular culture, the Taj Mahal has become a global icon, appearing in films, television shows, advertisements, and even music videos. Its instantly recognizable silhouette and the story of love that it represents have made it a popular motif in romantic films and literature. The Taj Mahal's image has been used to evoke a sense of timeless beauty, exoticism, and mystery, and it has become a symbol of India itself in the global imagination. This cultural significance has further amplified the monument's influence on art and architecture, as its image continues to inspire creative interpretations in various forms of media.

The Taj Mahal's lasting influence on art and architecture can also be seen in the ongoing efforts to preserve and protect the monument as a cultural and architectural treasure. In the decades since its construction, the Taj Mahal has faced numerous challenges, including environmental degradation, pollution, and the pressures of mass tourism. Conservationists and architects have worked to ensure that the monument remains structurally sound and that its artistic features are preserved for future generations. These efforts have not only helped to protect the Taj Mahal itself but have also highlighted the importance of preserving other examples of Mughal architecture and Indian cultural heritage.

In conclusion, the Taj Mahal's influence on art and architecture is vast and multifaceted, extending from its immediate impact on Mughal architecture to its global legacy as a symbol of beauty, love, and cultural synthesis. Its innovative use of symmetry, balance, and decorative artistry set a new standard for architectural excellence in India, inspiring countless buildings, artworks, and designs in the centuries that followed. The Taj Mahal's unique blend of Islamic, Persian, and Indian elements, combined with its emotional resonance as a monument to love, has made it a source of inspiration for architects, artists, and designers around the world. Whether through direct emulation or through the incorporation of its underlying principles, the Taj Mahal's enduring legacy continues to shape the way we think about beauty, architecture, and the power of cultural fusion in the arts.

Chapter 16: UNESCO World Heritage Site

The Taj Mahal, one of the most iconic monuments in the world, earned its status as a UNESCO World Heritage Site in 1983. This prestigious recognition is not only a mark of its extraordinary beauty but also a testament to its immense cultural, historical, and architectural significance. The decision to include the Taj Mahal on this list was influenced by several important factors that make the site remarkable and worthy of international protection and appreciation. Each of these factors adds to the complexity of the monument, enriching its value beyond the visual marvel it presents to visitors from around the globe.

First and foremost, the Taj Mahal stands as an exceptional representation of Mughal architecture, a style that flourished in India between the 16th and 18th centuries. The Mughal Empire was known for blending architectural influences from Persia, Central Asia, and local Indian traditions, and nowhere is this synthesis of styles more breathtaking than in the Taj Mahal. This fusion of design elements results in a structure that is incredibly harmonious and symmetrical, combining domes, minarets, gardens, and reflective water bodies in a way that creates a sense of balance and serenity. The materials used in the Taj Mahal also contribute to its UNESCO status. The gleaming white marble is inlaid with precious and semi-precious stones like jade, crystal, lapis lazuli, and amethyst, which form intricate floral and geometric patterns. This type of inlay work, known as pietra dura, is one of the hallmarks of Mughal artistry, and the Taj Mahal exemplifies the peak of this technique.

In addition to its architectural brilliance, the historical and cultural significance of the Taj Mahal is immense. Built by Emperor Shah Jahan in memory of his beloved wife, Mumtaz Mahal, the Taj Mahal is often regarded as the ultimate symbol of love. The depth of emotion behind its construction elevates it beyond mere architecture into the realm of poetry and human sentiment. The story of its creation is both romantic and tragic, as it commemorates a love so profound that it inspired the emperor to build one of the most magnificent structures in the world. This narrative contributes to the global appreciation of the monument and its legacy, which spans centuries. People from all cultures and walks of life are drawn to the universal themes of love, loss, and devotion that the Taj Mahal embodies.

Another key reason why the Taj Mahal was recognized as a UNESCO World Heritage Site is its historical context and the role it plays in reflecting the political, social, and artistic landscape of the Mughal era. The Mughals were known for their passion for the arts, and under Shah Jahan's reign, architecture reached new heights. The Taj Mahal is often seen as the culmination of this period of cultural flowering, representing the zenith of Mughal artistic achievement. Moreover, the complex history of the Mughals, their interactions with various cultures, and their lasting influence on India's architecture and society are encapsulated in the Taj Mahal. This rich historical backdrop contributes to the site's global significance, as it offers insight into one of the most important empires in the history of the Indian subcontinent.

The setting of the Taj Mahal also plays a role in its UNESCO designation. The monument is situated on the banks of the Yamuna River in Agra, India, in a beautifully landscaped garden that follows the traditional Charbagh, or four-part garden layout. This layout, which was popular in Persian and Mughal architecture, symbolizes paradise and is meant to evoke a sense of order, peace, and divine beauty. The entire complex is designed with symmetry in mind, and the placement of the Taj Mahal at the northern end of the garden, rather than the center, creates a stunning visual effect, particularly when viewed from the entrance. The reflection of the Taj Mahal in the central water channel adds to its ethereal beauty, making the monument appear as though it is floating in space. The careful integration of the building with its surrounding landscape enhances its aesthetic value and contributes to the overall sense of harmony and perfection.

The preservation and safeguarding of the Taj Mahal have been ongoing efforts, which also contribute to its standing as a UNESCO World Heritage Site. Over the centuries, the monument has faced various challenges, including environmental pollution, structural degradation, and the pressures of tourism. In response, the Indian government, along with international organizations, has implemented numerous measures to protect and restore the Taj Mahal. The monument's inclusion on the UNESCO list has helped raise awareness about the importance of conservation and the need to maintain the integrity of the site for future generations. UNESCO's involvement has also brought in global support, ensuring that the Taj Mahal remains protected from the threats it faces in the modern world.

The Taj Mahal's significance as a UNESCO World Heritage Site extends beyond its architectural and historical value. It is a symbol of India's rich cultural heritage and plays an important role in the country's identity on the global stage. For many people around the world, the Taj Mahal is the quintessential representation of India, and it continues to be a source of national pride. As one of the Seven Wonders of the World, the Taj Mahal draws millions of visitors each year, contributing significantly to India's tourism industry and economy. Its status as a World Heritage Site ensures that it will continue to be recognized and celebrated as a global treasure.

In summary, the Taj Mahal's designation as a UNESCO World Heritage Site is due to a combination of its architectural splendor, historical importance, cultural symbolism, and ongoing preservation efforts. It represents the pinnacle of Mughal architecture and stands as a monument to love and loss, resonating with people from all corners of the globe. Its beauty, symmetry, and intricate craftsmanship are unmatched, making it one of the most visited and admired monuments in the world. The Taj Mahal's enduring legacy, its influence on Indian and world architecture, and its representation of a significant period in history all contribute to its status as a site of universal value. Its protection under UNESCO ensures that future generations will continue to marvel at its beauty and appreciate the rich cultural and historical narratives it represents.

Chapter 17: The Restoration and Preservation of the Taj Mahal

The restoration and preservation of the Taj Mahal are critical efforts that have spanned centuries and involved numerous challenges, as the monument's enduring beauty and historical significance demand constant attention. Maintaining a structure as large and intricate as the Taj Mahal requires ongoing care, especially considering the many factors that threaten its stability, appearance, and integrity. From the moment it was completed in the mid-17th century, the Taj Mahal has faced natural wear and tear, environmental pollution, and the pressures of millions of visitors. Despite these challenges, extensive preservation measures have been implemented to ensure that this iconic symbol of love remains as pristine as possible, enabling future generations to continue to marvel at its grandeur.

One of the most significant challenges in preserving the Taj Mahal is the natural aging of its materials. The Taj Mahal is primarily constructed from white Makrana marble, a highly prized stone that gives the monument its luminous appearance. However, marble is not impervious to the effects of time, weather, and pollution. Over the years, the white marble has gradually yellowed, primarily due to air pollution from the surrounding area. Agra, the city in which the Taj Mahal is located, has experienced significant industrial growth over the past century, leading to an increase in air pollutants like sulfur dioxide and nitrogen dioxide. These pollutants react with the marble, causing it to discolor and develop a layer of grime, diminishing the building's signature white glow.

To address this issue, numerous cleaning and restoration techniques have been employed over the years. One of the most effective methods used in recent times is a treatment known as "multani mitti," which is a type of fuller's earth clay. This clay is applied to the marble surface and allowed to dry, drawing out impurities and pollutants from the stone. Once the clay dries, it is carefully washed off, revealing a cleaner, whiter surface underneath. This method has been applied to the Taj Mahal's exterior multiple times, restoring much of its original brilliance. However, the process must be conducted with extreme care, as excessive cleaning could damage the marble. Balancing the need to preserve the Taj Mahal's aesthetic beauty with the importance of not harming the structure itself is a constant concern in restoration efforts.

Another major issue facing the Taj Mahal is structural stability. The monument, including its enormous dome and four towering minarets, sits on the banks of the Yamuna River. While the river provided a picturesque setting for the Taj Mahal, it has also posed significant risks to its foundation. Over the centuries, the flow of the river has shifted, and the water levels have fluctuated, leading to concerns about the stability of the Taj Mahal's foundations. The monument was built on a complex system of wells and wooden foundations designed to absorb the shock of minor earthquakes and maintain the building's balance on soft ground. However, as the Yamuna River's water levels have decreased due to environmental changes and human intervention, there are concerns that the foundations could weaken over time. To prevent potential damage, experts have suggested measures such as recharging the river with water to maintain the necessary moisture levels for the wooden foundations to remain stable.

Additionally, the minarets that frame the Taj Mahal have shown signs of tilting over time, further raising concerns about the long-term stability of the structure. This has led to detailed studies and surveys using modern technology like laser scanning and ground-penetrating radar to monitor the condition of the foundations and the overall stability of the monument. By regularly assessing the building's structure and identifying potential weaknesses, preservation experts can implement necessary interventions before any serious damage occurs.

The threat of environmental pollution continues to loom large in the ongoing preservation of the Taj Mahal. In addition to the air pollution that has caused discoloration, the nearby Yamuna River is heavily polluted, which affects not only the riverbanks but also the surrounding air quality. The Indian government has taken several steps to reduce pollution in the vicinity of the Taj Mahal, including establishing a large buffer zone around the monument called the Taj Trapezium Zone. This zone restricts industrial activity and the use of certain fuels in order to reduce harmful emissions that could damage the Taj Mahal. Factories that release pollutants into the air have been either shut down or relocated farther from the site, and restrictions on vehicle traffic near the Taj Mahal have been implemented to lower exhaust emissions.

The efforts to reduce pollution are complemented by international collaboration. The Indian government, working alongside international conservation organizations and UNESCO, has sought to implement sustainable practices to ensure the long-term preservation of the monument. UNESCO's involvement has been crucial, as it provides both technical expertise and global awareness of the need to protect the Taj Mahal. Experts from around the world have contributed to research and restoration projects, bringing a wealth of knowledge and innovative solutions to address the myriad challenges the site faces.

In addition to environmental and structural challenges, the Taj Mahal must also contend with the impact of tourism. As one of the most visited landmarks in the world, the Taj Mahal attracts millions of tourists each year. While this influx of visitors is crucial to India's tourism industry, it also places a great deal of strain on the monument itself. Foot traffic, touching of the marble, and the general wear and tear caused by such large numbers of people can lead to the gradual deterioration of the site. In response, the Indian government has implemented strict regulations on visitor behavior. For example, there are limits on the number of visitors allowed inside the monument at any given time, and areas of the Taj Mahal that are more vulnerable to damage have been roped off to prevent people from touching the marble.

Despite these efforts, managing the balance between welcoming tourists and protecting the monument is an ongoing challenge. The demand to see the Taj Mahal remains high, and as more people travel to Agra, especially during peak tourist seasons, the pressures on the site increase. Authorities are constantly reviewing and adjusting policies to ensure that tourism does not compromise the long-term preservation of the Taj Mahal.

Another aspect of the Taj Mahal's preservation is the ongoing maintenance of its gardens and surrounding landscape. The Taj Mahal is part of a larger complex that includes expansive gardens designed in the Persian Charbagh style. These gardens, with their carefully laid-out walkways, reflecting pools, and fountains, are integral to the overall aesthetic and spiritual experience of the site. Maintaining these gardens requires constant attention to ensure that the plants, trees, and water features remain healthy and in line with their original design. Over the centuries, the gardens have undergone various changes, with some sections being modified or replanted. However, recent efforts have focused on restoring the gardens to their original Mughal-era layout, as they were intended to represent paradise on Earth. This restoration of the gardens is not only about preserving the visual beauty of the Taj Mahal but also about honoring the cultural and religious symbolism embedded in the monument's design.

The preservation of the Taj Mahal is a continuous process that requires a multi-faceted approach. From cleaning the marble to monitoring structural stability, from reducing pollution to managing tourism, each aspect of preservation demands careful planning and execution. Moreover, the challenges faced by the Taj Mahal are not static; they evolve over time as environmental conditions change and new threats emerge. The involvement of national and international organizations, combined with modern technology and historical knowledge, has been crucial in safeguarding the monument.

Ultimately, the restoration and preservation of the Taj Mahal are about more than just protecting a beautiful building. The Taj Mahal is a symbol of India's cultural heritage, a reminder of the Mughal Empire's artistic achievements, and a universal representation of love and devotion. Preserving this monument ensures that it continues to inspire awe and admiration for generations to come, reminding the world of the incredible skill, creativity, and human spirit that went into its creation. The story of the Taj Mahal's preservation is a testament to the global effort to protect our shared cultural treasures and ensure their survival in the face of modern challenges.

Chapter 18: The Stories of Visitors to the Taj Mahal

The Taj Mahal, often referred to as the "Crown of Palaces," has been captivating visitors for centuries. Its grandeur and intricate beauty inspire admiration, curiosity, and awe in everyone who stands before it. But the stories of the visitors who have come from all corners of the world to see this magnificent structure are as diverse and interesting as the monument itself. Whether it's a historical figure, a world traveler, or an everyday tourist, each visitor to the Taj Mahal brings their own perspective, experiences, and emotions. These stories form a rich tapestry that adds to the monument's legacy, making the Taj Mahal not just a structure of stone and marble, but a living symbol of human emotion, ambition, and wonder.

Historically, the Taj Mahal attracted the attention of rulers, explorers, and chroniclers from distant lands. One of the earliest notable visitors was François Bernier, a French physician and traveler who served in the Mughal court during the reign of Emperor Aurangzeb. In the 17th century, just a few decades after the Taj Mahal's completion, Bernier visited Agra and was awestruck by the monument. He documented his impressions, marveling at the sheer scale, elegance, and beauty of the structure. Bernier's accounts introduced European readers to the wonders of Mughal India, and his descriptions of the Taj Mahal helped fuel Western fascination with the East. His observations were among the earliest accounts of the Taj Mahal that circulated in Europe, spreading its fame far and wide.

In the centuries that followed, countless other travelers from across the globe made their way to the Taj Mahal, each leaving behind stories of their encounters with the monument. For some, the visit was part of a larger journey through India, a land that had long fascinated the Western world for its exotic allure, its wealth, and its mysterious culture. British travelers, in particular, were drawn to the Taj Mahal during the period of colonial rule in India. Many British officers, administrators, and their families visited the site, often writing about the powerful emotional impact it had on them. The grandeur of the Taj Mahal, coupled with its romantic backstory, resonated deeply with them, and for many, it became a symbol of the wealth and complexity of the Indian empire they governed.

One particularly touching story is that of Lord Curzon, a British viceroy of India who served in the early 20th century. Curzon was deeply moved by the Taj Mahal and took an active role in its preservation. At the time, the monument had suffered some neglect, and parts of it were in disrepair. Lord Curzon initiated extensive restoration work, ensuring that the Taj Mahal was properly maintained and cared for. His personal connection to the monument was so strong that he even commissioned the restoration of the gardens and installed a marble lamp inside the mausoleum in memory of Queen Victoria. Curzon's story reflects how deeply the Taj Mahal could affect those who came into contact with it, regardless of their background or position in life.

For many visitors, the Taj Mahal is more than just an architectural marvel – it is an emotional experience. The love story between Emperor Shah Jahan and Mumtaz Mahal, for whom the Taj Mahal was built, touches the hearts of people from around the world. Numerous visitors arrive at the monument with a sense of reverence, knowing that it represents not only one of the greatest achievements in architecture but also a symbol of eternal love. One common story is that of couples who visit the Taj Mahal as part of their honeymoon, seeing it as the ultimate romantic destination. For them, the monument becomes a personal symbol of their own love and commitment, mirroring the undying devotion that Shah Jahan had for his wife. The sight of the Taj Mahal at sunrise, bathed in the soft glow of the early morning light, has left many couples deeply moved, making it a memory they cherish for the rest of their lives.

However, not all stories associated with the Taj Mahal are romantic. For some visitors, the monument evokes a sense of melancholy and reflection. The story of Mumtaz Mahal's death during childbirth and Shah Jahan's subsequent grief adds a layer of sadness to the experience of visiting the Taj Mahal. Many visitors are struck by the contrast between the monument's beauty and the tragic circumstances that led to its construction. Some have described their visit to the Taj Mahal as a meditative or spiritual experience, where the quiet reverence of the place allows for deep reflection on life, love, and loss. The stillness of the marble, the symmetry of the gardens, and the soft echo of footsteps in the mausoleum create an atmosphere that encourages contemplation, and many visitors leave feeling a sense of peace and introspection.

Over the centuries, the Taj Mahal has also attracted the attention of artists, poets, and writers, whose stories have further enriched the monument's legacy. Rabindranath Tagore, the famous Indian poet and Nobel laureate, famously described the Taj Mahal as "a teardrop on the cheek of time," capturing the monument's delicate beauty and its emotional depth. His words have been quoted by countless visitors who feel the same sense of wonder and sadness when they see the Taj Mahal. Writers and poets from around the world have also used the Taj Mahal as a source of inspiration, seeing in it a universal symbol of love, loss, and the passage of time. These artistic interpretations of the Taj Mahal add to the rich narrative surrounding the monument, turning it into a cultural and emotional touchstone for people across the globe.

In the modern era, the stories of visitors to the Taj Mahal have become even more varied and diverse, reflecting the monument's status as one of the most recognizable landmarks in the world. Today, people from all walks of life and from every corner of the globe make their pilgrimage to Agra to see the Taj Mahal. Social media has amplified the reach of these stories, with visitors sharing photos, videos, and personal reflections about their time at the Taj Mahal. For many, the opportunity to see the monument in person is a lifelong dream come true. The sight of the Taj Mahal often exceeds their expectations, leaving them speechless at its scale and beauty. These stories, shared across platforms like Instagram, Twitter, and travel blogs, help to keep the Taj Mahal's legacy alive, allowing people who have not yet visited to experience the monument vicariously through the eyes of others.

But it's not just foreign tourists who have stories to tell about their visits to the Taj Mahal. For many Indians, the Taj Mahal holds a special place in their hearts as a symbol of their country's rich cultural heritage. School groups from across India visit the Taj Mahal as part of educational trips, learning about their country's history and the Mughal era through the lens of this magnificent monument. For many young visitors, seeing the Taj Mahal in person after reading about it in their history books is a profoundly memorable experience, instilling a sense of pride in their cultural heritage. Families from all over India visit the Taj Mahal to admire its beauty, often incorporating the trip into larger pilgrimages to other important sites in the country.

The stories of visitors also include moments of personal significance, such as proposals, anniversaries, or family reunions. There are countless anecdotes of people proposing marriage in front of the Taj Mahal, seeing it as the perfect backdrop for such a meaningful moment in their lives. Others visit the Taj Mahal to mark special anniversaries, celebrating decades of love in a place that was built in honor of one of history's most famous love stories. Families separated by distance have also used the Taj Mahal as a meeting point, making their reunion even more special by sharing it in such an iconic and beautiful location.

Among the most poignant stories of visitors to the Taj Mahal are those that reflect personal journeys of healing and closure. Some people visit the monument after experiencing loss in their own lives, finding comfort in the story of Shah Jahan and Mumtaz Mahal and in the beauty of the structure itself. The Taj Mahal's association with both love and death creates a space where visitors can process their own emotions, often finding solace in the quiet reflection that the site encourages. The peaceful gardens, the gentle breeze from the Yamuna River, and the timelessness of the white marble create an atmosphere that fosters emotional healing for many visitors.

In conclusion, the Taj Mahal is much more than a monument of stone and marble; it is a living, breathing symbol that continues to inspire, move, and affect people from all over the world. The stories of the visitors who have come to the Taj Mahal, from historical figures to modern travelers, form an essential part of its legacy. Whether it's the story of a British viceroy who helped restore the monument, a couple celebrating their honeymoon, or a family gathering for a reunion, each visitor adds their own chapter to the long history of the Taj Mahal. These stories, filled with emotion, wonder, and admiration, ensure that the Taj Mahal remains not only a marvel of architecture but also a testament to the enduring human spirit. As long as people continue to visit, the Taj Mahal will continue to inspire new stories, each one adding to the monument's rich and ever-growing history.

Chapter 19: Discovering the Yamuna River by the Taj Mahal

The Yamuna River, flowing beside the Taj Mahal, plays an integral role in the overall setting, history, and significance of one of the world's most iconic monuments. The relationship between the Taj Mahal and the Yamuna River is not merely geographical but deeply symbolic and intertwined with the cultural, environmental, and historical context of the Mughal era. Shah Jahan, the Mughal emperor who commissioned the construction of the Taj Mahal, intentionally placed the monument along the riverbank, enhancing its aesthetic beauty while adding a layer of spiritual and practical significance. Discovering the Yamuna River in the context of the Taj Mahal provides insight into the reasons behind its location, its impact on the monument, the challenges it poses today, and how the river has been a silent witness to centuries of history, serving as both a lifeline and a symbol of India's past.

The Yamuna River is one of India's most important and sacred rivers, second in spiritual significance only to the Ganges. Originating from the Yamunotri Glacier in the Himalayas, the river flows through several northern states of India, passing through the cities of Delhi, Mathura, and Agra, before merging with the Ganges at Allahabad (Prayagraj). In Hindu mythology, the Yamuna is considered the sister of Yama, the god of death, and is believed to have the power to purify sins. The river has long been central to the lives of people who settled along its banks, including the Mughal emperors, who established their grand cities near the river to take advantage of its fertile lands, transportation routes, and spiritual resonance.

When Shah Jahan chose the site for the Taj Mahal, the Yamuna River played a pivotal role in his decision. The location offered several practical benefits, such as providing a stable water source for the construction and future maintenance of the monument. The river helped cool the palace gardens and the surrounding area, a crucial consideration given the hot climate of northern India. In addition to its practical advantages, the river's proximity gave the Taj Mahal a serene and reflective quality. On a clear day, the monument's white marble façade casts its image into the waters of the Yamuna, creating a mirror-like reflection that enhances its ethereal beauty. This sense of perfect symmetry was central to the Mughal architectural aesthetic, and the river became a vital part of that design.

The placement of the Taj Mahal beside the Yamuna River also has a deeply spiritual and symbolic meaning. In Islamic tradition, gardens and water are often symbolic of paradise, and the layout of the Taj Mahal's complex was designed to evoke the image of a heavenly garden. The Charbagh, or four-part garden that surrounds the monument, is divided by water channels that represent the rivers of paradise. By positioning the Taj Mahal beside the river, Shah Jahan aimed to create a sense of eternal beauty and tranquility, with the flowing waters of the Yamuna serving as an earthly reminder of the spiritual rivers that run through paradise. This connection between the river and the monument helped Shah Jahan fulfill his vision of the Taj Mahal as a place of eternal rest and beauty, not just for his beloved wife Mumtaz Mahal, but for himself as well. After his death, Shah Jahan was buried beside her in the mausoleum, with the Yamuna River standing as a silent guardian to the monument and the legacy of their love.

The Yamuna River also played a crucial role during the construction of the Taj Mahal. The vast quantities of marble and other materials needed to build the monument were transported along the river. In an era where modern roads and infrastructure did not exist, rivers served as the primary means of transportation for heavy materials. Boats and barges ferried enormous slabs of marble from quarries hundreds of miles away, as well as other building materials like sandstone, jade, crystal, and precious metals. The river's role as a transportation route allowed the construction of the Taj Mahal to proceed efficiently and helped facilitate the creation of one of the most impressive architectural feats of the Mughal era.

As the years passed, the Yamuna River continued to be an important element of the Taj Mahal's surroundings. The river sustained the lush Mughal gardens, which were designed to bloom year-round, showcasing a variety of plants, flowers, and trees. These gardens were an integral part of the experience of visiting the Taj Mahal, offering visitors a peaceful, verdant environment where they could reflect on the beauty of the monument and its symbolism. The flowing river provided the necessary moisture to maintain the plants and trees, creating an oasis-like atmosphere in the otherwise arid region of Agra.

However, as time progressed and the demands of modern life increased, the relationship between the Yamuna River and the Taj Mahal began to face significant challenges. Rapid urbanization, industrial development, and pollution in the surrounding areas have taken a heavy toll on the river. The Yamuna, once a clean and vibrant waterway, has become heavily polluted, with untreated sewage, industrial waste, and agricultural runoff being dumped into its waters. This pollution has had serious consequences for the health of the river's ecosystem, affecting not only the plants and animals that rely on it but also the appearance and stability of the Taj Mahal itself.

One of the major threats posed by the polluted Yamuna River is its impact on the Taj Mahal's marble. The chemicals and pollutants in the river and the surrounding air can contribute to the discoloration and degradation of the monument's marble. In recent decades, the Taj Mahal's once-pristine white marble has taken on a yellowish hue in some areas, a result of the combined effects of air pollution, acid rain, and contaminants from the river. Conservation efforts have been undertaken to clean the marble and restore its original brilliance, but the ongoing pollution of the Yamuna remains a persistent problem that threatens the long-term preservation of the monument.

The shrinking water levels of the Yamuna River also pose a threat to the stability of the Taj Mahal's foundations. The monument was built on a complex system of wells and wooden foundations designed to absorb shock and maintain stability on the soft ground. These wooden foundations require moisture to remain intact, and the drying up of the Yamuna River has led to concerns that the foundations could weaken over time. If the river continues to recede, it could potentially cause the monument to shift or sink, leading to structural damage. Efforts have been made to address this issue, including proposals to replenish the water levels of the Yamuna through artificial means, but finding sustainable solutions has proven to be a complex challenge.

In recent years, environmentalists and historians have called for greater efforts to clean up the Yamuna River and restore it to its former glory. They argue that preserving the river is not only essential for the health of the local ecosystem but also crucial for safeguarding the future of the Taj Mahal. The Indian government, along with various international organizations, has launched several initiatives aimed at reducing pollution in the river and implementing more sustainable water management practices. These efforts include better waste treatment facilities, stricter regulations on industrial pollution, and public awareness campaigns to encourage responsible waste disposal. Although progress has been slow, there is growing recognition of the need to protect the Yamuna River for both environmental and cultural reasons.

The Yamuna River's historical and cultural significance cannot be overstated. For centuries, it has been a lifeline for the people of northern India, providing water for drinking, irrigation, and transportation. It has also been a sacred river in Hinduism, with countless myths and religious rituals associated with its waters. For the Mughal emperors, the Yamuna was a source of inspiration, and it played a pivotal role in shaping their architectural and urban designs.

The river not only sustained their cities but also served as a symbol of power, beauty, and eternity.

The interplay between the Yamuna River and the Taj Mahal also extends beyond the physical realm into the realm of art and imagination. Many artists, poets, and photographers have drawn inspiration from the sight of the Taj Mahal reflected in the waters of the Yamuna. The image of the monument, mirrored perfectly in the calm surface of the river, has become one of the most iconic and enduring images in the world of photography. Poets and writers have also been moved by this image, using it as a metaphor for the fleeting nature of life, love, and beauty. In this way, the Yamuna River continues to add depth and meaning to the Taj Mahal, both in the literal sense of its reflection and in the symbolic sense of its association with timelessness and the flow of history.

Despite the challenges posed by modern development and environmental degradation, the Yamuna River remains an essential part of the Taj Mahal's story. Efforts to restore the river and protect the monument are ongoing, and there is hope that future generations will continue to be able to experience the beauty and tranquility of the Taj Mahal as it was originally intended – with the Yamuna flowing serenely beside it, offering a quiet reflection of the monument's white marble splendor. In many ways, the story of the Yamuna River is a reminder of the delicate balance between nature and human achievement, and the need to protect both in order to preserve our cultural heritage for future generations.

In conclusion, discovering the Yamuna River by the Taj Mahal is not just about appreciating the natural beauty of the river itself but also about understanding its profound influence on the history, architecture, and spiritual significance of one of the world's most treasured monuments. The Yamuna River is a thread that weaves through the story of the Taj Mahal, connecting the monument to the broader cultural and environmental context of India. Whether as a source of inspiration for Mughal architects, a lifeline for the city of Agra, or a reflection of the Taj Mahal's ethereal beauty, the Yamuna River is an essential part of the Taj Mahal's identity, and its preservation is crucial to ensuring that the legacy of this wonder of the world endures for generations to come.

Chapter 20: The Taj Mahal in Popular Culture Today

The Taj Mahal, a timeless symbol of love and architectural brilliance, has transcended its historical and cultural origins to become an enduring icon in popular culture today. While it was initially constructed as a mausoleum by Mughal Emperor Shah Jahan in memory of his beloved wife Mumtaz Mahal, the Taj Mahal has evolved into a global cultural phenomenon, widely recognized for its aesthetic beauty, romantic associations, and symbolic significance. Its presence in popular culture is vast, spanning films, music, literature, fashion, art, and even global diplomacy, making it one of the most celebrated and referenced monuments in the world. To understand the magnitude of the Taj Mahal's impact on modern popular culture, it is essential to explore its representation across different mediums, its symbolism in global affairs, and its role in inspiring creativity and artistic expression.

One of the most prominent ways in which the Taj Mahal has cemented itself in popular culture is through its appearance in film and television. The monument has been featured in countless movies, ranging from Bollywood blockbusters to Hollywood productions, and its visual splendor continues to capture the imagination of filmmakers worldwide. In Indian cinema, the Taj Mahal is often depicted as a backdrop for romantic scenes, symbolizing eternal love, much like its historical origin. Films like *Taj Mahal* (1963), directed by M. Sadiq, explore the emotional depth of Shah Jahan and Mumtaz Mahal's love story, while movies like *Mughal-e-Azam* (1960), one of India's most celebrated historical dramas, reflect the grandeur and opulence of the Mughal era, with the Taj Mahal serving as a symbol of the cultural and architectural achievements of that time.

In international films, the Taj Mahal has appeared in various contexts, often serving as an exotic and breathtaking location that underscores the monument's global recognition. In *Slumdog Millionaire* (2008), the Taj Mahal is portrayed not only as a tourist attraction but also as a reflection of the cultural and social disparities in modern India, where local children attempt to capitalize on the influx of foreign visitors. Similarly, the Taj Mahal was featured in the 2012 James Bond film *Skyfall*, where the monument, though briefly shown, is used to evoke the elegance and mystique of India as part of a high-stakes international adventure. The presence of the Taj Mahal in these films is not incidental; it carries with it the weight of history, romance, and majesty, which filmmakers use to heighten the emotional and visual impact of their storytelling.

Television, too, has not been immune to the allure of the Taj Mahal. Countless travel documentaries, history programs, and reality shows have showcased the monument as an essential stop for anyone exploring the wonders of the world. Programs like *The Amazing Race*, a reality competition show that sends contestants around the globe, have included the Taj Mahal as a key destination, further embedding it in the consciousness of audiences worldwide. The monument's appearance in popular media reinforces its status as one of the most recognized landmarks globally and enhances its cultural mystique as a place where history, love, and beauty converge.

The influence of the Taj Mahal in music is another fascinating aspect of its role in popular culture. While not as frequent as its cinematic appearances, the Taj Mahal has been referenced in various musical compositions, particularly in songs that explore themes of love, loss, and devotion. In the West, several songs have drawn on the monument's symbolism to evoke feelings of romantic longing or to illustrate the grandeur of a powerful emotional connection. One famous example is the song *Taj Mahal* by Jorge Ben Jor, a Brazilian musician, whose lyrics reference the love story behind the monument. The Taj Mahal has also made appearances in music videos, adding a touch of exoticism and grandeur to visual storytelling. Its beauty and history make it a powerful metaphor for love and loss, which musicians continue to draw upon when crafting their works.

Beyond its presence in entertainment, the Taj Mahal has also become a potent symbol in global diplomacy and international relations. World leaders, dignitaries, and royalty often make a point of visiting the Taj Mahal when traveling to India, and these visits are widely covered by the media, further enhancing the monument's status as a symbol of goodwill and cultural diplomacy. For instance, when Princess Diana visited the Taj Mahal in 1992, she famously posed alone in front of the monument, a photograph that quickly became iconic. The image of Diana, alone in front of a monument built to honor love, became a poignant representation of her troubled marriage with Prince Charles. The photograph not only solidified the Taj Mahal's association with love but also with personal introspection and melancholy, adding layers of meaning to its symbolism in popular culture.

Other notable visitors to the Taj Mahal include U.S. Presidents, British Prime Ministers, and global celebrities, each of whom contributes to the monument's ongoing legacy as a cultural ambassador of India. The Taj Mahal is frequently used as a setting for diplomatic photo opportunities, symbolizing both India's rich cultural heritage and the universal themes of love and beauty that transcend borders. The monument's role in these high-profile visits helps to reinforce its global significance and ensures that it remains a relevant and recognizable symbol of India on the world stage.

In the world of fashion and design, the Taj Mahal has also left a significant mark. Its architectural details, such as the intricate floral patterns and geometric designs found in the marble inlay work, have inspired countless fashion designers and artists. The monument's aesthetic has been incorporated into textiles, jewelry, and home décor, often as a way of channeling the elegance and sophistication associated with Mughal art. The use of white marble as a design motif, combined with the floral and geometric patterns seen in the Taj Mahal's décor, has been replicated in fashion collections and art installations, allowing the monument's visual language to transcend architecture and enter the realm of contemporary design.

In the realm of literature, the Taj Mahal continues to be a source of inspiration for writers, poets, and novelists. Rabindranath Tagore, one of India's most celebrated poets, famously described the Taj Mahal as "a teardrop on the cheek of time," capturing the monument's melancholic beauty and its connection to the themes of love and loss. This poetic description has since been widely quoted and has become emblematic of how the Taj Mahal is perceived in the collective imagination – as a symbol not just of romantic love, but of the passage of time, mortality, and the transient nature of human emotions. Countless novels, essays, and poems have been written about the Taj Mahal, each attempting to capture its essence or explore its historical significance. From historical fiction that delves into the lives of Shah Jahan and Mumtaz Mahal to contemporary novels that use the monument as a metaphor for human relationships, the Taj Mahal remains a fertile ground for literary exploration.

The monument's influence also extends to contemporary visual art, where artists from around the world have drawn inspiration from its form and meaning. Painters, photographers, and sculptors have used the Taj Mahal as both a subject and a muse, creating works that range from realistic depictions to abstract interpretations of its symbolic significance. The monument's symmetry, scale, and attention to detail make it a favorite subject for artists, while its associations with love and loss give it a depth of meaning that transcends mere aesthetics. In modern art galleries and exhibitions, the Taj Mahal often appears as a symbol of India's cultural heritage, but also as a universal representation of beauty, love, and the fragility of life.

The impact of the Taj Mahal in popular culture also extends to the realm of tourism, where it has become one of the most visited and photographed landmarks in the world. Millions of tourists flock to Agra every year to witness the beauty of the Taj Mahal firsthand, making it a global pilgrimage site for travelers from all walks of life. The advent of social media has amplified the Taj Mahal's presence in popular culture, as visitors share their experiences through platforms like Instagram, Facebook, and Twitter. The iconic image of the Taj Mahal – often captured at sunrise or sunset when its marble façade glows in the soft light – has become one of the most recognizable and frequently shared visuals on social media. This digital proliferation has helped to keep the Taj Mahal relevant in contemporary culture, as new generations of travelers and photographers engage with the monument in creative and personal ways.

In addition to its role as a tourist destination, the Taj Mahal has also been commercialized in various ways, from souvenir shops selling miniature replicas of the monument to luxury hotels offering views of its iconic silhouette. Its image is used in advertisements, travel brochures, and promotional campaigns, capitalizing on the universal appeal of its beauty and historical significance. The Taj Mahal has become a brand in itself, representing not only India's cultural heritage but also the idea of romance, elegance, and grandeur. This commercialization, while sometimes controversial, has helped to solidify the Taj Mahal's place in the global consciousness, ensuring that it remains a relevant and beloved symbol in modern culture.

In conclusion, the Taj Mahal's influence in popular culture today is vast and multifaceted. It appears in films, music, literature, fashion, art, and global diplomacy, each time carrying with it the weight of its historical significance and its universal symbolism. Whether as a backdrop for a romantic film, an inspiration for a work of art, or a setting for diplomatic photo opportunities, the Taj Mahal continues to captivate the world's imagination. Its beauty, elegance, and emotional depth make it a symbol that transcends time and place, ensuring that it remains one of the most iconic and celebrated monuments in the world. As long as people continue to engage with its story, marvel at its architecture, and be moved by its symbolism, the Taj Mahal will remain an indelible part of popular culture for generations to come.

Epilogue

You've now journeyed through the wonders of the Taj Mahal, discovering its rich history, stunning architecture, and the fascinating stories that make it so special. From the love story of Shah Jahan and Mumtaz Mahal to the incredible craftsmanship of the workers who built it, the Taj Mahal is much more than just a beautiful monument. It's a symbol of India's past, a masterpiece of art, and a place that continues to inspire people around the world.

As you close this book, remember that the Taj Mahal is not just a structure frozen in time. It lives on through the visitors who marvel at its beauty, the historians who study its origins, and the millions of people who cherish its story. Whether you someday stand in front of it in person or continue to explore it from afar, the Taj Mahal will always remain a testament to the power of love, imagination, and human achievement.

I hope this journey has sparked your curiosity and filled you with wonder. The Taj Mahal is just one of many incredible monuments in the world, but it's a reminder that history is filled with stories waiting to be uncovered. Keep asking questions, keep exploring, and keep learning, because the world has so much more to offer.

Thank you for joining me on this adventure. The Taj Mahal will always be here, ready to welcome you back whenever you want to relive its magic!

The End.

www.ingramcontent.com/pod-product-compliance
Lightning Source LLC
Chambersburg PA
CBHW051230160726
47994CB00002B/819